15 HOT TIPS
that will

SUPERCHARGE

Your Sales Career

by CARL HENRY

Cover and book design by Alex LaFasto

First Printing 2008

ISBN 978-0-9657626-1-8

For Will and Virginia

Contents

Acknowledgements

Hardly any accomplishment is ever truly an individual triumph. While there's often one person who makes the winning speech, gets the big award, or finds their name on the cover of the book, the truth is that the success is almost always a team effort. And for that reason, acknowledgements are often more notable for who has been forgotten or overlooked, than for whose contributions have been recognized.

With that in mind, I'd like to pass on trying to name each single person that I owe my success to, and simply extend my sincerest thanks and gratitude to *everyone* who has made this book, and my career, possible. Without the constant and continuing support that I received, I wouldn't have been fortunate enough to learn everything I'm sharing in this book.

From my clients and colleagues who have kept me going all of these years, to my family and friends who have cheered me on, know that I'm grateful to all of you.

> **Great salespeople** *have an* exceptional understanding *of their craft.*

Introduction

Many years ago, I was a new producer, as I know many of my readers are, cutting my teeth on my first commission sales jobs. Through a great deal of trial and error, and then mostly more error, I found that there were certain truths in sales – that is, techniques that could be learned and duplicated. And so, I eventually moved into the realm of a sales coach and educator. It meant a bit more work, but I've gotten the opportunity to see those tools that I learned, organized into The MODERN Sales System, implemented and used around the world.

Not only have I been able to see lots of places and meet thousands of interesting people, but I've received a great deal of recognition and the satisfaction of knowing that I've helped so many others to find their fortunes. In each thank-you card, letter and follow up phone call, I got to hear stories of producers who doubled their income and veterans who were re-energized. I even heard from a handful of younger salespeople who, about to leave their sales careers behind, gave it one more shot and used my system to become top performers. Some of them have done so well that they've moved up to management and are leading their own sales teams now. It would seem that I'd done my part. Or so I thought.

After using and teaching The MODERN Sales System for the last couple of decades, I realized that I was still learning and growing. Following my seminars, clients and students came back with assorted questions, or asked what else I could teach them. In this process, I realized that I had pieces of advice that I hadn't included in my original book. They weren't exactly part of The MODERN System, but built upon it. I originally thought of adding them to my first book. But as soon as I began to put them on paper, I recognized that there would be too much to throw into an already complete title. I realized then that it would be time for a bit more work.

The result of that work is the book you hold in your hands: *15 Hot Tips That Will Supercharge Your Sales Career*. In it, you'll find all of the things that I couldn't tell you the first time around. You'll learn not only how to get more from your prospecting, qualifying and closing, but also a great deal about the best way to approach, and grow, your sales career.

If you've never read The MODERN Sales System, don't worry. Everything in here will make just as much sense as it would have otherwise. In fact, I've even included a short primer on the system and its advantages in one of the chapters. If, after reading and profiting from the advice in this book, you decide that you'd like to give MODERN a try, I invite you to get a copy and see what it can do for your sales career.

Now, with all of that out of the way, let's see if we can't turn my hard work into a bigger paycheck for you. Let's get started...

" Great salespeople *are accountable for their own success. They don't blame others or expect anyone to do it for them.* **"**

Do You Have the Right Attitude to Supercharge Your Sales Career?

E very once in a while, specials are run on TV about 'one hit wonders,' bands who rocketed up the charts with a single song and then faded away. The circumstances around the chart-topper are different. Sometimes it's a catchy tune, a physically attractive group, or a lyric that catches on with the public; but regardless of their appeal, the reason for their downfall is always the same. In every case, they weren't able to duplicate their success because their follow up work was terrible.

Contrast that with the bands that seem to have defied logic – not to mention medical science – by hanging around forever. Look past the party scenes and drunken mayhem and you'll notice a few things: they work hard, know that each album is a process, go the extra mile to please their fans, etc. The point is that even in the ultra-competitive world of music, anyone can stumble across a bit of luck and find a bit of success, but to really succeed takes a lot of hard work over a long time that isn't always outwardly apparent. Sales is no different. There will always be people who will come into the industry looking to make a quick buck with a bad gimmick, and a few of them might even make it for a while. But in sales, there are no lip-synched performances, no studio magic, and no backup singers to hide behind. Pretenders are always exposed. This book is about how not to be a one hit wonder in sales.

With that in mind, it's important to ask yourself if you really want to be in sales in the first place, and why. If you think you're going to fake your way to an easy paycheck, then do yourself and your employer a favor and walk away now. It's just not going to happen for you. But if you're in it because you want to make as much money as you can without going to school for decades or testing the bounds of the law, then this book is going to show you exactly what you need to do to succeed.

Nothing in these pages is magic, and some of it might not even be that new, but I can promise you two things: that everything you read will be clear and proven true. I can show you how to make it to the top, but you have to want it in a way that will drag you out of bed and to your office, to your phone and to your meetings, every single day.

A big mistake that many salespeople make is thinking that they have a real job. Well, they don't. In a real job, you show up at the office at a specified time, do your job well enough not to get fired, and then get a predetermined sum of money for your troubles. This is not going to happen in sales. In many cases, you aren't going to receive anything outside of what you earn selling. And even if you are getting some kind of base salary, it's likely to be less than you'd make if you spent your time bagging groceries at Safeway or playing a guitar on the sidewalk. It's going to be up to you to decide how much to put into your career, and how much to get out of it.

So I'll ask again. Why are you in sales? I don't care if you've been in it for three days or thirty years. If you don't have an answer that will make it worth the hard work and the ups and downs that come with a sales lifestyle, then you're going to be disappointed with what I, or anyone else, can teach you. If you don't want to do this, then don't. You can fake a lot of things in life, but a desire to sell isn't one of them. When it's just you and a phone or a prospective client, there is nowhere to hide. You must want it with a passion. If you don't, it isn't going to be worth your while.

With that disclaimer out of the way, sales is a great career. In fact, I think it's the best job there is, and I can't imagine why anyone would want to do anything else. And if you work at it the right way, it will reward you handsomely.

If you really want to be a top producer, then everything you'll need to get started is in the following chapters. As I said before, I can't make you want to sell, but I can show you the way if you do. By learning from my experience you can knock years off of the learning curve and jump to the next level. It doesn't matter if you're brand new or a seasoned vet. I only ask that you try to get as much out of it as I've tried to put into it. The information and advice that I'm about to give can make you millions a year, as it has for others, or it can give you nothing. It all depends on you. Don't let this book die on your shelves. Read through it once, and then from time to time, read it again. Hang on to it and use it as a resource when you need a reminder.

I've been in sales long enough to know what works. If you do everything in this book and aren't successful, then you aren't doing everything in this book.

You have to have

FUN.

You can't prosper in this job unless you truly enjoy it.

Excerpted from *High Energy Sales Thoughts: 101 Positive Sales Thoughts and Ideas* by Carl Henry

"Whether it's nature

or nurture, top producers
almost always share a single common
natural trait —*desire.*"

The DNA of a Great Salesperson

Early in my sales training career, I thought that I could turn just about anyone into a successful salesperson. It seemed like a simple formula: take a strong product, find an ambitious person, mix in some training, and '*Voila!*' out comes a great career and a healthy bottom line.

Over the years, however, I have noticed a large divergence in my seminar attendees. On the one hand, many of them – even some that were previously considered poor performers – went on to become sales superstars who broke company records and set the bar higher than it had been before. In fact, some moved into management or training themselves and became some of my best clients. But others couldn't find the same success. How could this be? They came from the same companies, sold the same products and received the same training. Why should they fall when their colleagues soared?

The question intrigued me for a long time. I gave some long thought to factors that I hadn't considered at first glance. Perhaps the high achievers were smarter, or had received a superior education. Or, maybe they had a personal life or family connections that would more easily lend themselves to a sales mindset. None of these answers felt right, but I was searching for a clue that seemed just beyond my grasp.

Luckily, I found that I wasn't alone in wondering why some salespeople succeeded and some didn't. My search led me to Target Training International (TTI), a behavioral research firm, and I've been working together with them ever since. Founded by analyst Bill Bonnstetter, the group looked into the hidden causes of achievement in the sales field, with an eye toward predicting those who would flourish against those who would fade.

The issue seems strikingly simple, but a simple poll of sales managers across the country would serve as a testament to the difficulty in finding, much less predicting, sales success. Ask any one of them who have sat through year after year of interviews, and they'll tell you a stark truth: hiring for sales – arguably the most important piece of a company, the only

department that brings in new money and customers
– is basically a hit and miss game. Even after making
educated guesses relating to background, education,
past experience and so on, more new salespeople
will fail than will succeed. And out of those who make
it, only a small handful will go on to be top earners.

With little else to go on, most sales managers prefer to hire good-looking, articulate personnel in the
hopes that their magnetism will translate into productive numbers. Bill became convinced that there must
be more to the equation. He recognized that a salesperson's underlying attitude and beliefs might be a
stronger determining factor than their waist size or jaw
line. But how does one measure things like desire and
mindset? Since it's impossible to take stock of those
things directly, he began by focusing on behavior, the
one area that can be observed. By taking note of a
person's behavior in enough areas and situations, he
could gain a keen insight into their real motivations.

Instead of testing applicants and seeing how well
they did their jobs, he started by testing top performers from different industries. Only men and women
who could clearly be defined as exceptional were included, to be sure that the behaviors would accurate-
ly reflect those who were doing well, not people who
were simply hanging on to their jobs. The idea was
not to find out who could make a living at sales, but
rather who was truly excelling at sales. Over years

of study, he discovered how successful salespeople work and react in certain situations, and then tested those observations. In other words, he decided to see what people who were succeeding were doing, and then designed a way to see if other people could succeed in the same way.

What he discovered was both obvious and profound. Put simply, there are a lot of people in sales who shouldn't be. This is possibly a strange thing to say in this book. After all, I've built my career on sales – first as a salesperson, and now in training others to do better. I think it's the greatest job in the world. But, this test further proves that it's not for everyone.

It turns out that not all of us have the right makeup for a sales career. There's nothing good or bad about this, it's just a simple fact of life. Some of us really were born to sell, and some of us are better served in other roles. It's part of our DNA. Don't believe me? Imagine we are staging a race. As competitors, we have setup a racehorse and a donkey. In such a head to head match up, the racehorse will beat the donkey every time, regardless of motivation or effort. The donkey can do everything right in his training and preparation, eat the right meals and get enough sleep, but will still stand no chance on race day. It's just the way he's made. It's his DNA.

I'm not suggesting that any of my readers are donkeys, only that we all have subtle, but different, ingredients that make up who we are. So what does it take to be a top salesperson? For starters, a love of money doesn't hurt. Time and again, in TTI assessments, we found that top producers were motivated by money. They like it and want more of it. Their goals are influenced by it. As soon as they taste it, they set about doing the same things to get more. As far as sales performance is concerned, a desire for money drives results.

While there are many things that job seekers look for – a fancy prestigious title, a friendly social atmosphere, terrific working conditions, an aesthetically pleasing space – highly productive salespeople reported again and again that they were not overly concerned with these things. Nearly three-quarters of them said that more than anything else, they wanted money. Money may be the root of all evil in theory, but it's also the root of most strong sales careers.

This makes sense, intuitively. After all, for someone looking to make a huge salary, sales is probably the best legal option. Of course there are other fields where big earners emerge, think legal, medical, etc. But these careers usually require extra and more tedious education and ultimately, might even present more intellectual than financial reward. Pound for pound, it's tough to beat sales as a way to fill up the bank account quickly.

So ask yourself, what motivates you? What is it that you really want? If you want to earn more money than you ever dreamed would be possible, you might be on the right track. If it's to travel to exciting places for business, see your name in the newspaper or look out your corner office window onto a picturesque landscape, then you might be in the wrong field. It's certainly possible to sell if money is not a big motivator for you, but just know that the odds are against you.

Another common denominator of successful salespeople is that they tend to be *utilitarian*. What does this mean? It means that they want to use whatever is at hand to get the job done. They aren't overly interested in technical details or abstract concepts. They just want the tools necessary to do the job, and then they want to get it done.

What if you're not a 'textbook' profile of a successful salesperson, but you still feel convinced that it's the career for you? Don't worry. Not every top producer has the same profile. There are as many ways to sell as there are to do anything else. What works for one may not work precisely the same way for another. Tastes and methods differ. For instance, there is a small, but noticeable group of analyzers who consistently show up as top sellers. These are the people who like to examine every angle of a problem, know every technical spec, and think about the questions behind the questions. As a rule, they make poor producers, but a few of them still manage to buck the trend and break out.

What is the lesson in this? Should we go back to saying that performance cannot be predicted? Absolutely not. We know from numerous studies over the decades that certain people will have a much easier time than others. If you don't have a traditional sales mindset, compensate for it. Work with your style and know where your weaknesses are. Find your strengths and use them in a way that will further your sales career, not hinder it. If you like to examine problems, use that as a way to fire up your presentations. If you like to get public recognition then translate that motivation into a desire to win sales awards. It doesn't matter exactly what you do, just know that you'll have to adapt your natural style to make it work for you.

Think about how the characteristics of top producers apply to you. Remember, there are no right or wrong answers. It's all about finding the right fit. When the job rewards your value structure, it's a good fit. If your goal is to make money, the best job to make money legally is to sell. If you have something else as your number one value, then the odds are that you won't sell. You might think you want to, but subconsciously, your mind has other values that it will defer to, day after day.

All of this is a heady way of saying that if you enjoy your work, it will be much easier for you. There is nothing new in this statement, so why do so many people find themselves mistakenly in sales? Because it's difficult to ask ourselves what we value and get honest answers. Many people don't really know what their underlying attitudes are. They may think that they're motivated by money because they want to be, but on a deeper level it isn't wealth they crave, it's power or attention. Again, there is nothing inherently wrong with these priorities. But if they go unrecognized, they can lead to a lot of frustration and regret.

If you're at all on the fence as to whether or not you belong in sales, give yourself an assessment. You can e-mail me directly at chenry@carlhenry.com to arrange one. The reports themselves are great, and I recommend one for everyone. It's like a high-powered x-ray device, except that instead of assessing bones, the assessments measure your attitudes, beliefs and core values. They look into who you are at ground level. Precise questions strike at the heart of your personality to find out what really drags you out of bed in the morning. Try it. You might find out some things about yourself that you didn't know and at the very least, you'll finish knowing where your strengths and weaknesses are.

Of course, having the right makeup for a salesperson doesn't ensure that you'll succeed. You might be born to sell, but that doesn't mean you know how to sell. Just as prize racehorses can lose to their competitors who are similarly suited to their roles, even the most natural salesperson can fail. Laziness, lack of technique or even the wrong product can turn a winner into a loser. This is where good sales training comes in.

Good training can also give you clarity and focus. Let me present an example, using a common situation at the Henry home. Suppose a Saturday morning comes around and the lawn needs to be mowed. It sounds like a simple problem, but without clarity and focus, I won't be able to get the job done. Imagine that I have no focus: I know how to mow the lawn, but it's not really a priority to me. Chances are, I'm going to watch a lot of baseball and the grass is going to grow for another day. Or, it could be that I'm focused, but not clear. Maybe my wife finally convinces me that the lawn really does need to be mowed, but I'm not sure what the weather will be like or if the mower is working. Once again, I'm missing a key ingredient and the lawn continues to grow.

The same principles apply to your sales career. Without clarity and focus you will never make it to the top of the sales ladder. Find out exactly who you are, and then tune your skills until you become the best. This chapter has been aimed directly at producers, but there are great lessons for sales managers as well. Taking the time to properly evaluate recruits can save you thousands or millions of dollars a year, not to mention the headaches that come with trying to fit a square peg in a round hole. When looking for new salespeople, look beyond the pressed suits and finely printed resumes. Look deeper and find out more about your candidates – use an assessment or other tool to find out what makes them tick. Keep hiring men and women with the right DNA, and they'll take you to the finish line consistently.

Do things that create

laaaaaaaaaaaasting

success. Take action today and you'll get something positive tomorrow.

Excerpted from *High Energy Sales Thoughts: 101 Positive Sales Thoughts and Ideas* by Carl Henry

> **If you want to be**
> a multi-million dollar producer,
> you need to think like one.

Thoughts of a Multi-Million Dollar Producer

People love sports heroes. Part of it, I think, is that they're natural entertainers. Week in and week out, we see them on television experiencing the full range of human emotions – from the highs of victory to the lows of defeat.

But more than that, the best of them give us a glimpse into the winning mindset. While the average athlete might look at a lopsided scoreboard and see a bad night, a winner sees a chance to make a dramatic comeback. In their mind, problems and obstacles become challenges to overcome. That's what makes them the best, and that's the reason that so many of us love watching them.

Salespeople aren't that different. In every office and in every industry, there are a few superstars that stand out above the rest. Some have natural talent, while some rely on experience and devotion, but they all approach their jobs with the same winning mindset.

If you want to join their ranks and succeed at their level, you'll need to develop the same kind of outlook in your own career. In this chapter, I've taken a few examples of their thinking. Notice how their minds are always geared towards winning. Yours should be too.

"Multi-million-dollar producers know that prospecting is a never-ending job. The secret is to leverage all contacts."

You can never stop looking for business. Just as a shark must swim or die, so it is for salespeople. Every day, clients move on to take different jobs, retire, or to give business to someone new. Without new customers, your business will eventually suffocate and die. It's so easy to put prospecting aside when we're already busy, but don't take the temptation. As full as your cupboard might seem today, without prospecting, you may soon find yourself with too much free time, struggling to find more people to sell to tomorrow. Take a bit of time to prospect each day. Your sales, not to mention your mind and your paycheck, will be steadier.

"If ten percent of the salespeople make 90 percent of the sales, who are you emulating? Associate with top producers."

Who do you spend your time with? Is it with top salespeople, or with middle-of-the-road producers who spend more time having coffee than they do selling? Because it's so easy to pick up the habits and attitudes of those around you, the company you keep is very important.

One of the easiest ways to make more money in sales is to start hanging out with others who are more successful than you. You'll probably find that they have a specific system that has led to their high performance – a system that you can duplicate in your own career. Besides learning their techniques, you might have a good time. Most multi-million-dollar producers are interesting, educated and motivated. Take one out to lunch and you will learn something.

"You will make many mistakes in your sales career. Making mistakes is a very expensive, but necessary, way to learn."

If you are new to sales, and even if you haven't been new for a long time, chances are that you are going to make some errors. Whether it's a botched presentation, a price negotiation that turns into a fiasco, or just a bungled sales call, you're going to screw something up. Some mistakes are minor, taking only a few minutes to get over. Others will ruin your entire week.

When the inevitable happens, you must be resilient. Learn from your mistakes, because they're the best teachers. When you miss out on a sale, ask yourself why, and then go over the situation in your mind until you're confident that you won't make the same mistake again. There's no substitute for experience, so be sure that you get the most out of yours – good and bad.

"Working for $12.50 an hour is boring. Making a $100,000 sale is exciting."

If you feel bored by what you're doing, the problem might not be your job; it might be your expectations for your job. When you come into work on Monday morning, what are you thinking about: making a few small deals and getting by, or taking steps towards the sale that's going to get you a summer home on the beach? Set your sights higher than you've ever imagined, and you'll have a much better time.

"Take a look in the mirror every once in a while and ask yourself, 'Have I prepared enough?' If the answer is 'No,' your sales career is in jeopardy."

If you aren't engaged in what you're doing, then someone else is going to eat your lunch. Take the extra time to be on top of your game. Know your product's specs, as well as those of your competitors. Be able to answer questions that your prospects are likely to ask, and counter foreseeable objections. You know when you're ready to work, and so do your customers.

"I have thought about quitting selling a million times, and then I call my friends with normal, secure, boring jobs. Well, maybe not secure—but definitely boring."

You're lucky to be in sales, don't ever forget that. Sure, there are going to be down days, but what would be the alternative? Where else are you going to find the freedom to do things your own way, a higher earning potential than nearly any other field, and the possible recognition of being a top performer?

Additionally, top producers enjoy the kind of job security that is virtually unheard of in today's economy. As companies slash jobs left and right, sending whole departments overseas or cutting them altogether, do you know who never gets laid off? A producing salesperson. Because sales is the only department that actively and directly brings in new revenue, its top performers are invaluable. Find me someone who is selling consistently, bringing new money in the door, and I'll show you the last person that a company will get rid of, and the first that another company will hire if given the chance.

"When you are clear and focused on something, it usually happens quickly. Get clear and focused in your sales career."

Top producers know exactly what they want – money and sales. They can't help but know, because they're thinking about it all the time. They've programmed themselves to be obsessed. It's no accident that successful salespeople seem so narrow-minded. They don't get distracted by what's going on around them, and as a result they get what they're reaching for much more quickly.

What is the first thing you think about when you wake up in the morning? What is it that gets you out of bed, the thing that you don't just want, but that you crave? Answer that question, and you'll go a long way towards finding out what kind of sales you're going to make.

"You don't go out and get a multi-million-dollar sales job; there is no such thing. You build a multi-million-dollar sales career."

Most people don't realize that it sometimes takes ten or more years of selling to become an "overnight success." Remember, selling is not a job, it's a career. If you want to make the big bucks, you're going to have to work at it, day after day. Take the long view – keep learning, keep prospecting, and keep sharpening your mind to sell.

"Nothing makes me happier than a happy customer who likes to talk."

A satisfied customer who is willing to sing your praises is worth his weight in gold. Go the extra mile and build a steady stable of these folks. Over time, they will help you close more sales than you'd be able to without them.

"You haven't made your biggest sale yet. There were a lot of times I was down, and the next day I made a big sale."

If you are always prospecting and closing the way that you should, you're never as far from a sale as you think. Just as the account that you were sure to close will sometimes disappear, others that you have written off will return from the dead. That's just the way it goes. Keep plugging away, and you'll be surprised to find how many sales will come 'out of nowhere.'

"Your past success does not guarantee your future success. Don't take anything for granted."

Yesterday's news is just that – yesterday's news. In this way, sales is somewhat like sports. We only get paid when we 'win,' that is, make a sale. It's great when you've made a big sale, and you should take a minute to celebrate and appreciate it. But after that, get back to work and start looking for the next one.

"It's more important to find the decision maker than the problem. The problem is easy to find; the decision maker is harder."

You can spend all the time you want explaining how your product is the answer that a company has been searching for. If your prospect has no power to buy, it's not going to do you any good. Take the time to find out who you're talking to and meeting with, before you invest a lot of time and energy in your presentation. If you aren't sure you have the right contact, ask them directly. It might be awkward, but it's going to save you a lot of work with someone who can't help you out.

"Most people don't get what we do for a living. Forget their ignorance and just sell something. It doesn't matter if they get it or not – it's your life."

From time to time, there are bound to be people in your life who don't understand your career. Usually, they are people in nine to five jobs, with a steady paycheck and the so-called security of a 'normal job.' They don't get the long hours, overnight trips and up-and-down pay scale.

So what? They don't have to. I believe that selling is the greatest profession in the world. It offers great pay, job security, and the kind of thrill that you can't find anywhere else. Sure, some people you know won't understand what you go through or why you do it, but they also can't get the extreme satisfaction that comes with closing a big deal. If sales suits you, live your life and have fun with it.

Do you want to be a millionaire? If you do, take these affirmations to heart and learn to think like one. If you don't, get out of sales and do something that you'll enjoy more.

Too many salespeople think *prospecting is the key to sales success.* **They're wrong.** *Successful prospecting is.*

Growing Your Sales

R ecently, I had the opportunity to conduct a seminar for INCA Flowers in Quito, Ecuador. A couple of days before the training, they offered me a tour of the grounds, which I gladly accepted. Our drive took us through acre after acre of the most striking, exotic flowers you could ever see, set against a lush, green terrain that seemed to drip with life. As a kid who grew up in New Jersey, the irony of the 'Garden State' seemed thick. Here I was, in the middle of this sort of earthly paradise I'd only expected to ever see on digitally enhanced postcards.

As the tour progressed, my host Sebastián Troya explained some of their processes and challenges to me. Mother Nature had provided an excellent environment for their gardening brilliance, but that didn't mean that there wasn't still a lot of work to be done.

In order to make more than a very meager profit, they had to go beyond just taking what sprung from the earth. Each area had to be cultivated very carefully, and specifically if they were going to get the kinds of eye-popping results that they'd become known for.

It was this process of cultivation that ultimately seized my attention. In essence, what they were doing, to an untrained eye, seemed to be haphazard and disorganized. A closer look, however, revealed the intricate detail with which they grew their flowers. From the time that they were mere seedlings, each was monitored, fed, and watered. Individual adjustments were made for sunlight, soil nutrients, water, and trimming, based on what would produce the most spectacular results.

I couldn't help but be impressed with their methods. Instead of just planting a bunch of fields and seeing what sprung up, they took a wiser approach. They got a much better product and a lot less hassle from their insight, and so can you.

You see, too many of us run our sales careers like a sloppy farm operation, cultivating potential customers at random instead of letting them develop in their own time and space. New clients are our lifeline to a brighter future, and yet we give little thought to bringing them in. We prospect poorly, and pay a hefty price because of it. But why should we be so bad at doing the one thing that can guarantee us a better future?

I think that part of it has to do with the way we perceive prospecting as a solitary, torturous activity. The very word has its origins in mining lore, bringing forth images of young men and women buried in dark caves with little light, hoping to scratch enough gold out of the earth to make a living before they succumbed to illness or injury. Doesn't that sound like the way most of us approach finding new clients? Pounding away at phone calls until we either lose our resolve or happen to find a small nugget hidden within our ever-deepening lists?

I know it's certainly what they taught when I was learning sales. Armed with nothing more than a phone and a public directory, we'd try to thrash our way into a successful close. The rationale was that if you made enough phone calls, you were bound to find someone who was interested in what you were selling. Sales is a numbers game, after all, or so we were told. There's a certain rationale in that line of thinking that isn't completely wrong, and if you're at the beginning of your career with no contacts or experience, it might be the best thing for you. If nothing else, cold calling will teach you to reach out to new people, get comfortable shaking hands or talking on the phone, and net you a few sales. But once you've gotten a few thousand dials and handshakes in your past, you start to realize a funny thing: most of the people on your list don't want to get those calls any more than you want to make them. Luckily, there's a much better way to find new customers.

There is no magic to prospecting. The aim is as it has been for thousands of years - to find new customers who might buy your products. It's a very simple concept that we make harder than it has to be. It doesn't matter if you reach out electronically, over the phone, or go door-to-door shaking hands. As long as it works, it doesn't matter how you meet people. But, as I will so many times in this book, I'm going to advise you to work smarter, not harder.

The key to successful prospecting is to become a specialist instead of a salesperson. Forget the mass approach, and focus your efforts on a few people that you want to work with. Think like a laser instead of a shotgun. Look for people who fit a specific profile, and not for 'some people who might buy from me.' At first glance, you might think this doesn't make sense. Why ignore most of your potential clients in the hopes of gaining a few?

The answer is that even though it's counterintuitive, you can often sell more by worrying about a few people instead of a lot. By only marketing to people that you actually want as clients, you save yourself some headaches down the road. But more than that, you can catapult your production in a short amount of time. By filling your rolodex with similar types of clients, you increase your marketing power and decrease your workload.

Imagine two real estate producers. The first prospects randomly, using phone numbers from a phone book. Assuming that the salesperson makes enough calls, they're going to sell, maybe even consistently, but what will his customer base look like? Most likely, he will have a collection of clients with differing backgrounds, interests, and tastes. Some will be younger, some older, some with children, and others without. A few of his clients might be looking for apartments in the city, while others might long to move out into the country. Some will prefer newer properties, while others will desire something more classic. Each situation will require a great amount of time and research if he is to make a sale. Essentially, the salesperson is forced into being a jack of all trades.

Now, suppose that his colleague has taken a smarter approach. Instead of prospecting among 'likely buyers,' she decides to look for a very specific type of client - young professionals seeking lofts in a downtown area. Instead of making dozens or hundreds of calls each day, she can gather new prospects in much less time and with much less effort. She will have a much easier time keeping up on the market, the properties available in her area, her prospects' common needs and objections, and so on. Moreover, because she's working with the same types of people again and again, there is an increased likelihood that her clients will refer her to their acquaintances.

As you can see, prospecting can become very easy over time, or it can remain a difficult task for your entire career. Work smarter. Find a segment of the market for your products, create an image in your mind of your ideal clients, and then reach out to them. It will mean doing more at first, but it will be worth it. By becoming a specialist, you'll make your career exponentially less aggravating.

For one thing, your prospecting calls will be easier. Instead of searching for just any buyer, you'll be able to make an offer that is more likely to be of interest to the other person on the phone. To stay with our real estate example, picture our first producer making his calls. Using names from a public directory, he calls one prospect after another, introducing himself and asking the other person on the line if they're interested in buying a new home. Most people are going to hang up before he finishes the first sentence, so chances are, it's going to take a long time before he finds someone who is in the market. And even if he does, he's set the table for a tough meeting. People don't naturally talk to strangers about buying a house.

Contrast that with our second producer. Armed with a list of prospects that she's gathered herself

based on age, income, location, or other good buying factors, her calls will be more individualized and
substantive. Her opening conversation, or voicemail
message, might go something like this: "Hello, Ms.
Johnson. My name is Jane Producer and I've worked
with several of your colleagues to help them find the
downtown loft they've always dreamed of. I special-
ize in working with young professionals, and would
love to sit down with you for a few minutes if you
could make time in the future." Which call would you
rather make? Which one would you rather receive?

Another side benefit of the laser approach is that
you increase your odds for a referral exponentially.
Most companies, and many communities, are close-
knit. By working with the same types of people over
and over again, you drastically increase the odds that
they will pass along your name to someone they know,
or at the very least, you can get recommendations
that will carry weight with your prospects. Remember that you are part of the prospecting package. The
more experience that you can show a potential client
you have with their type of situation, the more likely
you are to make it the next step closer to a sale.

With these benefits of a targeted approach in mind,
the first step is to identify the right prospects. Who
are the right prospects? They're people who are likely
to have an interest in what you're selling and are able
to afford it. This is an elementary idea, but don't miss

both parts. You cannot substitute either of those criteria. A prospect who can afford your product but has zero interest or use for it will never buy. A prospect who shows an interest in you and your product but hasn't the money or authority to buy is an even bigger problem. Not only will they take up a lot of your time, but they'll make you feel like you're making progress and string you along right up until the moment that they never buy a thing.

So it's essential that no matter what kind of prospecting it is, you begin with a good list. These days, there are a lot of types of lists out there, but I recommend starting with your own if you can. It's certainly possible to get names, addresses and more from published business directories, list brokers, and other public or easily accessible information. The problem with these lists is that they're like air, or any other public resource. Everyone has them, and everyone is using them. They offer no competitive advantage.

Your list of prospects is your claim. Don't follow the crowd into a depleted shaft. Make your own way into the wilderness and find a spot that you can own and work by yourself. This is a bigger problem in some industries than in others, but you never want to work from a list that has been run through by every one of your colleagues and competitors. By starting from an over-prospected list, you're putting yourself in a position to call on people who have already received so many calls that they're not going to listen to your offer no matter what you say. They've heard it all before and just don't want to be bothered by phone or in their office. Or worse, even if you manage to make a sale, you can't be sure that your new client is going to be constantly inundated with other offers. Neither of these situations are likely to bring you anything more than aggravation, and certainly will not result in a lasting success.

Building your own lists takes a lot of groundwork, but it can pay you back with years of strong production. You can give yourself a good head start by answering a few questions. Who are your dream customers? Where do they work? Where do they live? What do they do in their spare time? How did they meet the last salesperson in your industry who sold to them? Think hard about these questions, because the people that you choose to prospect to will end up making up your client base. Make good decisions and you'll end up with great customers. Skip over it, and you're putting your future income at risk.

Once you've narrowed it down to your ideal customers, the rest is easy. All you have to do is find them. Look at the companies they work for. Read their magazines and newsletters. Learn where they live and work, and then start taking down names. Google and other search engines are wonderful prospecting tools, as are alumni publications, newspapers, trade magazines, web pages, annual reports, and even people you know. Add a few names each day and make a file for them. Include basic information like names, numbers, and addresses, as well as anything else that you think might be pertinent. Did they go to the same college that you did? Live in your hometown? Note it all. You want to know each of your prospects as much as you legally can when you're calling them, so that you can craft a personalized message that will speak to their needs and desires.

Once you've made your lists, it's time for contact. Obviously, one of the easiest and most popular ways to reach out to prospects is by using the phone. Since it's the first weapon most prospectors use, I'm going to assume it's a staple in your business as well. If not, just keep in mind that all of the principles in this chapter apply no matter how you're reaching out. That being said, as a sales tool, the telephone has suffered for its own success. By that, I mean that people attach a certain stigma to cold calling because it's been overdone, and overdone badly. Caller screening and receptionists have given way to caller ID and other more sophisticated means of keeping unwanted callers away. What's the way through? Show them that you aren't an unwanted caller. Be excited about what you're doing, and let them hear it in your voice. Act like a professional, individualize your calls, and always lead with benefits. People don't hate sales calls, they hate unwanted sales calls. If you call someone and can help them to improve their business or their life, your call will always be welcome.

One area where lots of salespeople fail is when it comes to leaving messages. They spend a great deal of time thinking about what they'll say, but none on what to leave as a message. Be prepared. Lots of prospects won't pick up, either because they aren't there or because they're screening their calls. If you get their voicemail, go ahead and leave a message. Write down a note to read if you need to. Sound excited, be concise, and leave your number clearly.

Another good tip is to get to know your prospect's assistants and receptionists. More often than not, these are the people who will be answering your phone calls and e-mails. Your initial contact, as well as your early relationship with the prospect, will likely be governed by their impressions of you. Remember, aside from their own typically hefty workload, they're usually responsible for fitting twelve or fifteen hours' worth of work on their bosses' daily schedules. This means cutting out anything extraneous. In other words, if they are trying to prevent you from speaking with the person you'd like to meet, don't take it personally. It's their job. Simply be courteous, but persistent. Act like a professional and your time will come.

The key is consistency. Prospect all the time. Do it every day, even if you're sick, even if it's cloudy, and even if your favorite team is playing on television. Decide how many calls you'd have to make to open up a new account every week. Find out, and then make them. For every few dozen calls you make, you're going to get a mix of hot and cold leads. Some times you'll luck out and speak with a prospect that can barely wait to buy. Other times, it will be nothing but voicemail and no-thanks-not-interested. Just choose your prospects carefully to tilt the odds in your favor and keep plugging away.

This will be much easier if you keep track of your efforts. By simply writing down how many calls you've made on a certain day, you'll have a much easier time appreciating that you're making progress even when they don't seem to be going well. It's hard to be up for cold calling when the last fifteen people have shot you down. But by reminding yourself of the last time you hit pay dirt, you'll be more motivated.

Keep in mind that things change from week to week and month to month. For the prospects that are hot, you'll obviously want to schedule a meeting as soon as possible. But for those who aren't as interested, simply keep their file. You don't want to waste all that effort you put into finding them. Simply enter their information into a database or contact management program, and drip on them from time to time. How, you ask, do you drip on them? It's easy. Just think of our gardening friends and their seedlings.

Some will sprout right away; others will take years to come into bloom. The trick is just to keep feeding them until they're ready. Did you see an article that pertained to their business? Send a clipping. Are you putting on a seminar or informational setting? Forward a notice. Send them a card on their birthday, if you know when it is. Don't act like a stalker, but keep putting your name in front of them every once in a while and let them know that you want them as a client. It might take a while, but they'll notice. And, when they need something that you're offering, they'll probably at least give you a shot.

Prospecting can be fun, or it can be something to dread. The choice is entirely up to you, but if you follow the advice in this chapter, the hard part will already be over by the time you've picked up the phone. Reach out to just a couple of prospective clients each day, in a smart way, and you'll soon build a book of business that will last you for decades.

"What a thrill

it is

to sell something."

The MODERN Sales System

When I first started out in sales, things didn't go very well. I was having a hard time even getting people to talk to me, much less buy anything. It was very frustrating. I had the desire, motivation, and drive to succeed, but something was missing. For the first couple of years, I struggled to hold on, until I was finally able to discover the problem. I was selling without a plan. For that matter, I noticed that most producers and their managers weren't following a logical step-by-step selling system, either. It seemed that none of us had much direction. I didn't know how to move my prospects forward, and never once did any of my supervisors ask, "where are you in the selling process?" Instead, they would just want to know, "did you get the order?"

Once I realized what I was missing, it was amazing how quickly things turned around. It is remarkable what will happen to your sales career when you master a sales system. Not only will it skyrocket your income, but it will guarantee your employment as well. When you master a system, you'll always be able to sell, and there are always jobs for people that know how to sell.

I didn't invent selling systems. I only stumbled upon them, and eventually developed my own, out of necessity. Frustrated by my lack of production, I was self-motivated and started to read sales books and to attend seminars. At each training session, I listened to experts on prospecting, negotiating techniques, listening skills, and general motivation. I enjoyed most of them, but with each conference my frustration grew. The instructors taught me *what* to do, but they never taught me *when* to do it. Finally, I realized that a sales system would solve this dilemma by taking the mystery out of the process. I could know where I was in the sales process, understand where I was going, and what went wrong when I wasn't successful. It didn't take long to figure out that a sales system wouldn't guarantee my success every time, but did increase my odds tremendously.

It's amazing to me that any salesperson can even survive without having a good system. But the great thing about it is that once you master one, you can do a lot more than hang on; you can take your career to the multi-million-dollar level by helping you to focus on what your customers perceive as value. You would think that everyone would instinctively follow a logical process when selling something. It would make sense that, at least on a subconscious level, we'd have a plan to move forward. The truth, however, is that most producers skip steps with their prospects and clients. Fewer than ten percent of us actually follow a logical selling system at all. The result is that our work is unfocused. We miss sales that we could have made, and end up making deals at lower margins than we need to, effectively giving ourselves a pay cut every day.

To make sure that you're not missing out, I'm going to teach you my method, which I call The MODERN Sales System. 'Modern' is an easy word to remember and if you can memorize it, you can remember the sales system. The system, a product of many years of real-world sales experience, is broken down into six easy-to-learn steps designed to help you close more business. The techniques in the system have been field-tested and proven to work in any industry or country. The MODERN Sales System is truly a global phenomenon.

Remember, selling is a systematic process that has a beginning, middle and an end. Top producers are aware of that, and utilize a system to keep themselves and their prospects moving toward a close in an organized way. By doing this, they give themselves an enormous competitive advantage because so few of their competitors will do the same. Let's see how it works:

RULES FOR USING THE MODERN SALES SYSTEM

Let me start by laying out the two important rules for using The MODERN Sales System. The first is that you do not skip steps. As I mentioned before, most salespeople do not follow a logical value-focused sales system. They have a tendency to jump all over the place, rather than staying focused. This rule will prevent you from making that mistake. As you'll see, it is critical to follow them in the order that I present them. Try to pass over one, and you'll probably find yourself frustrated and with very few sales to show for your work.

The second rule is an offshoot to the first: if you are having trouble moving forward in the sales process, you should always go backward. For instance, the qualification step should always come before a discussion of price. Therefore, if the customer asked you for the price prematurely you would say something like: "Before I can give you the exact price I will need to ask you a few questions." This statement both indicates a desire to help the client find the right product, and more importantly, prevents you from going forward too soon in the sales process.

These two rules are critical, and if you can remember them, you should be able to master The MODERN Sales System. There is one exception that I should point out, however. If a customer offers to invest in your product or service at full price, then by all means, let them. Don't tell them "I can't take the order until we complete all the steps in The MODERN Sales System." Just take the order and tell them all about what they've purchased later.

Now, on to the steps of The MODERN Sales System:

Step One: Measure The Selling Situation

In the Measure step, you're on a first date. You want to get to know your customers by concentrating exclusively on them and making them feel comfortable. Like any good relationship, you want yours with your client to be based upon trust, respect, and understanding. You also want to uncover the personality styles of the buying powers, the people in the company that can make, or break the sale.

Step Two: Organize Your Client's Needs

As you move into the Organize step your goal is to uncover the dynamics of your customer's problems and discover their needs, wants, and concerns.

Most customers appreciate this straightforward approach and respect a salesperson that takes the time to find out what they really want. You should develop an excellent list of qualifying questions, needs, and wants. Each question should help identify whether or not your customer is in a position to buy from you now or in the future. They should also seek to uncover the customer's requirements and desires, and tell which products and services they prefer.

Needs and wants questions look for a deeper insight. Think about how some of these samples might help give you a better picture of what your customer is looking for: *What are some of your major problems? What would you like us to do for you that no one else can? What types of problems are you experiencing now?* While these are the kinds of questions that will give you the best answers, keep in mind that clients might be reluctant to answer them at first. If you sense hesitation, ask them if you can continue to query them. If they agree, be sure to take notes on a clean sheet of paper so that you'll be able to refer to them later. Make sure you have defined the key needs and overall problem before you move on to the next step.

Step Three: Demonstrate Your Solutions

In the Demonstrate step you show your customers how you can solve their problems. If you have really thought through their problems and you have what you feel is an excellent solution, then this part should be a natural extension of that conversation. Demonstrate your solution in a way that is directly related to the problem at hand and show your customer exactly what they're getting. In showing them value, focus on the needs you discovered during the Organize step.

Be confident that your solution is the best one for your customer, as the manner in which you present it is just as important as the solution itself. If you lack enthusiasm for what you're pitching, your customer will, too. Take the attitude that you're a valuable resource to your customers and that they need your help in solving their problems. That is why you get paid, and why they're buying from you. Pay close attention to details and keep asking yourself, "How can my products or services help my customers solve their problems?"

Step Four: Engage The Mind & Senses

Want to know one of the best ways to close more business? Stop trying to sell, and focus on letting your customer buy. It's a subtle difference, but one that's predicated on your customer feeling like they've arrived at a solution, rather than you throwing one to them. And that's what this step is all about.

In the Engage step you go beyond demonstrating your products and give your customers possession. You want them to feel like they already have what you're selling, to get an immediate sense of the benefits that they'd get from buying. One of the best ways to do this is to involve your customers physically and give them "hands-on" use of your product. For example, if you sell plastic pipe, valves or fittings, put it in their hands and let them feel the quality. If you sell cars, have the customer sit in the leather seats and feel the hum of the motor.

If your product doesn't lend itself to a physical demonstration, then engage other senses. Sights, smells, and sounds all contribute to a strong impression. Better yet, get your customer emotionally involved. Paint a mental picture of how they'll feel after they've invested. The more you can involve them with the sales process by activating their senses and emotions, the more you're going to sell.

Step Five: Review the selling situation and make sure the customer is satisfied with your solution

This one is easy. When you begin the Review step, allow your customers the opportunity to review your proposal and reflect on the benefits they stand to gain.

Most traditional sales methods tell us not to slow down in order to give customers the opportunity to think about what they're agreeing to. Not only is this somewhat manipulative, it's bad business and it's unnecessary. When you use The MODERN Sales System, you have no reason to rush your customers through the Review Step. As you go through this process, your customer's trust in you deepens because you're showing them that you have nothing to hide. This simple act is often overlooked, but it's also one of the most powerful. Take the time to explain things to your customers, and you'll find yourself with happier buyers and more repetitive business. Remember that you are building a sales career and not just trying to make a quick sale.

Step Six: Negotiate and Close the Sale

When closing, you want to work toward a win-win agreement. You accomplish this by overcoming objections, and then simply asking your customers to invest in your solution. At this point in The MODERN Sales System they don't need to be sold, they just need to be reassured that your product or service really has all the value you have proposed. Of course, some clients will always raise objections during the close because they want to negotiate. They know that many salespeople will reduce their price if they see any resistance at all. Other times, customers will object because they truly have concerns about your solution to their problem. Differentiating false objections from real ones requires practice. The best thing to do is use visual and verbal evidence to uncover the true nature of their statements. From there, you can decide whether to verbally tell them why they should move ahead or you show them on paper why your solution is best.

It's important that you be just as strong at the end of the selling process as you were at the beginning. Be prepared for your customers to try to negotiate with you. They have learned from your competitors, and maybe even from you, that most sales people cut their prices at the drop of a hat, so it's likely that they will try to save a little money by talking you down. Using the techniques in this book, you'll be prepared to meet them head on. For now, just remember that effective negotiators approach these situations as a collaboration rather than as a competition. They learn to turn objections into reasons to buy. Practice putting yourself in your customer's shoes, and you'll have an easier time bringing them around to your point of view.

Will The MODERN Sales System Work For You?

The MODERN Sales System is an easy to learn, step-by-step sales process that provides the foundation for a successful, productive sales career. Each step is designed to move you and your customers closer to the logical conclusion of any sale – a buying decision. Don't reinvent the wheel every time you meet with a prospect. Because the system gives you a specific formula for selling, both veteran and novice salespeople can drastically improve their productivity right away.

WHY THE MODERN SALES SYSTEM WORKS

- It is a value-focused sales system.
- It allows flexibility by blending the steps of the selling process.
- It helps salespeople organize and direct their energy toward their customers.
- It is a professional approach to solving problems and selling solutions.
- It focuses on your customers and concentrates on meeting their needs.

Keep in mind that it's not always about you. In addition to helping you make more money, The MODERN Sales System will help your customers find solutions to their problems. Helping people is an exciting and fulfilling experience. Don't hold back. If you believe in what you're selling, don't be afraid to get excited when you are meeting with your customers and explaining your proposal. You are performing a valuable service. A sales system is a wonderful tool, but it's no substitute for energy and enthusiasm.

As any salesperson can tell you, sometimes it really is a jungle out there. Luckily, there are people who can help you find the way.

Cultivating Coaches

Hardly any flag was ever planted without help. When explorers would arrive in new lands, one of the first things that they would do – before sending word to the king or queen, before gathering riches or even naming some place after themselves – is find a native guide. From Columbus and Coronado to Lewis and Clark, every conqueror and conquistador along the way relied on locals to help them find their way in a new place. For these explorers, having someone around who knew the lay of the land wasn't just a convenience, it meant the difference between living and dying. Guides could communicate and negotiate with tribes and villagers, tell them what was safe to eat, or give valuable warnings like 'that swamp is filled with alligators.' With the right introduction, you were the guest of honor at a grand feast. Without it, you might find yourself as the main course. Your sales career is no different; it's good to have someone who knows where the alligators are.

Let me give you an example from my own career. Brooke Sykes used to work for a company that I did a series of training sessions for, dating back more than a dozen years. He had been with this particular firm more than 35 years, and knew the ins and outs like the back of his hand. No department, no product area, no relationship within the firm was outside of his knowledge.

As I worked with Brooke, he began to help me understand the intricacies of his organization. Time and again, he steered me toward the right person to sign off on a project, showed me who to call to be sure I could get the equipment I'd need for my presentation, or where to direct my invoices. His help made my relationship with this firm easier than it would have otherwise been. There is no way that I, as an outside salesperson, would have been able to figure out how such a large company ticked on my own. But through his assistance, I delivered dozens of programs to hundreds of their people over the years. It was a natural win-win for both of us. I continued to get more work, while Brooke was credited with having the foresight to bring in quality training for the staff.

From working with Brooke, I learned the importance of having a local on your side. When facing a large group, don't try to figure out everything on your own. Within every company you work with, or want to work with, there is someone who is intimately familiar with its inner workings. Look for a person who can show you the ropes and guide you in the right direction. These are the people who know the people, and can point the way. Cultivate coaches from your customers.

What makes a good coach? For starters, they must have a deep knowledge of the group or company that you're trying to infiltrate. They need to be connected and know the people that you will sell to, the people who will ultimately decide whether or not to buy from you.

It also helps if they're respected within the organization. This is just good common sense. After all, you're going to be counting on your coach to suggest you for future work, and any recommendation that they make for you is going to be exactly as strong as their reputation. If their colleagues think that they do a great job and generally make good decisions, then they'll probably listen when your coach sings your praises. On the other hand, if your coach is better known for sleeping at his desk than he is for spotting talent, his word might not get you very far. Make sure that your coach has a good reputation, or you might find that yours will suffer as well.

In the beginning, you'll have to work hard to come up with coaches. When you're new to your prospects, no one knows you or likes you. But keep reaching out, and eventually you will start to make contacts. Cultivating coaches is different than prospecting or customer service. Instead of digging around for new prospects, you're just trying to establish a better relationship with customers that you already know and like.

Most coaches come from satisfied customers. Think about the people you do business with. Are there any that you connect with especially well? Do you consider them to be friends as well as clients? If they're known and respected within their company or industry, they're probably a good candidate. As your career moves along, you should take special care to build these relationships. Work with your clients and show them that you're willing to go the extra mile. Make it easy for them to like and respect you as well. It might take dozens of calls and lunches, but it's worth the effort. The more coaches you have in your corner, the easier your life will become.

Having a coach in an organization can make all of the difference. When the discussion comes around on what to purchase or whose services to use, the squeaky wheel will indeed often get the grease. Put another way, in any group decision, it is often the person who wants it the most who will get their way. If your coach believes in you and your work, they will not only be a strong endorsement, but one coming from a voice that is known and respected by his or her coworkers. From there, it should be easy for you to break in and make a sale.

A good coach can not only get you in the door, but can also help you leverage your way into multiple sales and a long-term relationship with a company. They can even move you along into new ground and introduce you to more clients. The wonderful thing about people who are connected is that they tend to be connected beyond their own walls. When someone has been working in the same company or industry for a long time, they are bound to come into contact with suppliers, competitors and even their own customers - all groups of people that might be interested in buying from you on the recommendation of a friend.

To cultivate your coaches, rely on steady communication. When they meet with you, whether it's in person or over the phone, listen carefully to what they say. Get to know them and their interests, both at work and away. Make a phone call or take them out to lunch. Keep an open eye for anything you see that might interest them. If you come across a book or article that you think could help them do their jobs better, pass it along. If you discover something new in their business, let them know. Don't be annoying, but become a valuable source of information while letting them know that you appreciate the time and input that you've received. Early in my sales career, I learned a trick that's served me well. If I read something that seemed unique or interesting, I forwarded it to the coaches on my list. If it was an article, I made copies and sent them. If it was a book, I bought multiple copies and sent those. This simple act only took a few minutes here and there, but it was a steady reminder that I wanted to work with my coaches and wanted them to share in my success.

You might be wondering why a coach would take the time to help you. It's basic psychology at work. There is a simple and innate need for people to want to help others. If your coaches know you and like you, they're going to want to give you a hand. This is, of course, dependent on doing strong work. All of the reminders, and all of the lunches in the world, won't be able to help you if you don't treat your job like a profession or do sloppy work. As always, quality and hard work are a salesperson's best friends. Give your coaches a chance to brag about your performance and you'll go a long way toward opening new doors.

Cultivating coaches shouldn't be a one-way street. Just as your coaches can help you, be willing to help them as well. More than anything, you want your coach to succeed. When you do good work for them, they in turn look good to their peers for having made a smart decision. If they recommend you to someone else, give 110 percent. Let your coach look like a hero for making the good call. The praise that they'll receive will be motivation to recommend you again. In addition, your coach might move on to a higher position. The farther they go, the greater their influence and decision making responsibilities will be, meaning more work for you. Besides, any relationship should be give and take. If someone is willing to put in the time and effort to help your career, do the right thing and help them, too.

All of this might sound familiar to you, and it should. It's very close to the concept of relationship selling – the idea that people like to do business with people that they know. There is a feeling that after decades of use in companies around the world, relationship selling is dead. *The modern competitive age killed it,* they say, *now it's all about the product, the price, and the bottom line.*

Those people are only half right. The old days, if they ever existed, when you could take a customer out on the town and make sales by showing him a good time, are gone forever. Your skills and products must be able to stand on their own. If your customers don't see the value in what you're selling, they'll look elsewhere for lower prices, and if you don't deliver, the best relationship in the world won't matter. But in this competitive world we live in, relationships are more important than they ever were. When your clients like you and trust you to give them quality work at a fair price, then you'll be able to circumvent the competition before it gets in the door.

The modern world hasn't killed relationship selling, it's enhanced it. Cultivate coaches and take care of their needs – it's a simple way to give yourself a raise while making your job easier. When you move into a coaching relationship, you move beyond selling. You and your client are in it together. The normal trials and objections are replaced with trust. You become sounding boards and confidants to one another. You no longer have to beat each other up over prices and terms, because you can be confident that you're looking out for each other. Isn't that what every salesperson, and every client, should be aiming for?

You don't have to do anything unusual to cultivate coaches. Instead, you should just make a point to do what comes naturally – doing great work for people you like, and then keeping in touch with them. Coaches are just lifetime allies, mentors and friends. Remember that, and the rest will take care of itself. When you connect with a customer beyond the sale you are moving into a coaching relationship. It just starts with doing a great job. When you exceed your customer's expectations and they are one hundred percent satisfied with your product or service, you have planted a seed that can grow from customer to coach.

Don't

over**estimate**

your own sales ability or

un**estimate**der

your competitor's.

Excerpted from *High Energy Sales Thoughts: 101 Positive Sales Thoughts and Ideas by Carl Henry*

> **When you teach your customers** why your concept is the superior solution to their problem, *you increase your chances* of making a profitable sale and you frustrate your competition.

Sell the Concept First

My lifetime friend Len Kloeber is a West Point graduate and sales expert. I've known him for many years both personally and professionally, dating back to our first entrepreneurial experience—collecting carriages and hustling for tips at a local grocery store in northern New Jersey. After graduating from college I started selling real estate. Len ended up in the industry as well, working his way through law school by selling real estate franchises. Through the years, we stayed friends as both of our careers took off.

One afternoon, many years later we were discussing his accomplishments in the business arena, and he shared with me one of the secrets of his success – selling the concept first. He went on to explain that a concept is the intellectual generic version of a product that provides a solution to your client's unique needs, rather than the specific branded product that you are representing. His experience had taught him the importance of this idea, which had helped him grow his business for so long.

The premise was simple, and Len executed it to perfection while marketing his real estate franchises. He would meet with brokers, explaining franchising as a superior solution to the problems of advertising, recruiting and training agents, not to mention attracting buyers and sellers of real estate. Only when the broker had bought into the concept of franchising as an answer, and only then, did it make sense to start explaining the features and benefits of his specific franchise product. If they hadn't accepted the philosophy behind franchising, then they would never buy into his specific brand, the franchise company he represented.

Think about how this idea affects your own buying choices. In every purchase you make, you've bought into one concept or another. Suppose you decided to move into a larger house, and needed to find movers to transport your furniture and things. As you look into various options to get the job done, two salespeople come to your home. The first offers the services of a couple of workers who drive a large truck. The company name is "Two Clumsy Ex-Cons With An Old Truck" and their motto is "Nobody

Moves You Cheaper." The second salesperson also has strong workers that drive a large truck. Their truck features air ride suspension and their drivers are bonded and drug-tested. In addition, they offer certified packers and written guarantees of satisfaction. Their motto is "A Full Service Mover That Always Exceeds Your Expectations".

As a homeowner, if you only want the cheapest price, the concept of "Full Service" will be hard for you to swallow. The extras will likely be more expensive, and it will be difficult for the salesperson to justify their price to you. Even though paying a bit more for a certified packer that will virtually guarantee that grandma's antique dishes will arrive safely, that promise will fall on deaf ears.

On the other hand, if you're more concerned about the safety and condition of your home and belongings, you will be more receptive to the concept of full-service movers. You might not mind doling out a few extra dollars for the peace of mind that they offer. But it's only if and after you see value in their approach that you will be willing to commit money to their services. Now, the full service organization is a superior solution. If you accept that concept first it will be easier to be sold on the extra cost of the certified packer.

As a salesperson, it would be hard to overstate the importance of this simple idea. Until your customers buy into the concept of your product, be it safety, reliability, or something altogether different, telling them about various features is probably a waste of your time.

This power of concept selling can be applied to almost any industry. As an example, consider automobiles. If someone is sold on the concept of fuel-efficient personal transportation on demand, then they would be open to hearing a sales pitch for a small, fuel-efficient car. On the other hand, they would not be inclined to listen to someone selling an SUV, minivan, or pickup trucks since these vehicles represent an entirely different concept in transportation. It will be difficult to sell the concept of a gas-guzzler when the customer wants fuel-efficiency.

There are dozens of reasons why people buy cars, and getting from one point to another is only the beginning. Knowing this, dealers don't just sell vehicles with sturdy windshields or thick tires; they offer products that coincide with their customers' philosophies of what a car should be. If a salesperson offers an auto that doesn't evoke these responses, the customer will be reluctant to buy.

The same holds true for financial services. If someone understands the concept of life insurance as a way to provide for your family in the event of an untimely death, then they will listen to any salesperson that has a reputable life insurance product. Regardless of the specific policy, term or whole life, the sales person who helps them understand the concepts will have a tremendous advantage over other life insurance agents. They will have built a trust relationship with the client by focusing on their needs while selling the philosophy of safety and protection. The brand becomes a secondary sale, and a simple one, assuming that the agent is backed by a reputable firm.

You might think that concept selling doesn't apply to your business. It's easy to see the connection when a product is personal, like investment portfolios or moving services. But what if you're selling business-to-business? It would be easy to think that business-to-business products would sell themselves on price alone. And it is true that if you don't sell your superior concept, price will usually become the deciding factor for most customers. However, in this setting, selling the concept doesn't become less important, it becomes more important. Everything that is bought and sold has a concept or idea behind it. Even nuts and bolts are more than they appear.

One of my clients happens to sell industrial tooling and assembly systems. Their equipment is used to assemble automobiles and other industrial products around the world. By using computer sensors, they are able to tighten bolts with precision, ensuring that metal and other materials are fastened correctly every time.

It might be enough if they only made stellar tools, which they do. But they've taken their concept further. They know that quality is only half of the equation for their buyers. It's important that their tools work well, but it's even more important that they be working, period. With this in mind, they've developed a system of scheduled reliability maintenance that they sell along with the tools, ensuring that their customers won't face costly downtime. Not every customer appreciates, or even needs, the value offered in the scheduled reliability maintenance. Some smaller shops operate on a 'run to failure' model, opting to save money on the purchase and simply calling a repairperson when the tools break. Others simply see the guarantee as another expense that can be cut from the budget. Their concepts don't match the company's.

At this point, the salesperson has a choice to make. They can take the time to try to explain their superior concept to the customer and hope that they'll come around to the same point of view. If the customer cannot be convinced, they might be able to make a sale without the reliability maintenance. Or, if that option is not available, then they may simply walk away from the sale and work on finding new prospects that will understand and appreciate the concept that is being offered. But it's important to understand that it is only when both parties are seeing things the same way that anything will be bought and sold. The salesperson's challenge is to sell the superior concept first. When they accomplish this, the customer benefits and the competition is usually frustrated.

Adopting a concept selling approach is simple. The first step is to view your product or service from the customer's point of view. Consider the benefits that would come to them by buying a superior solution from you, and then take the thought a bit further.

If you aren't sure what they would be, then go straight to the source. Find an existing customer, or even a competitor's customer and throw out a few questions about what they really need out of your products or service. What in their eyes would be a superior solution? You might be surprised to find that the concept you're selling isn't the one they're buying. You may find that your concept is perceived as too expensive or revolutionary. The concept of portable computers was once thought too radical. Today everyone has computers. How would you like to be the salesperson that sold the first computers? They had to sell the concept first.

The benefits of this approach are huge. At the most basic level, it allows you to put yourself in co-operation with your customers, rather than be positioned against them. Once you show that you truly understand their needs, they will be more open to using your services as a solution. In the same way, price becomes less of an issue when customers are convinced that their jobs or lives can be improved by your goods. Cultivate enough buyers who see you as a resource and you will see your income skyrocket as your customers no longer see you as a salesperson but as someone who offers a superior solution.

It's only after you've connected with your customer on the concept level – the idea of something that will better themselves or their business – that the details of your specific product or brand will make any sense as a solution. If your customers aren't buying into your products on the concept level, you have a decision to make. In the short term, you can either try to help them understand the philosophy behind what you're doing, or you can simply hope to make a sale by negotiating on price. I always encourage selling your value and not your price. In the long term, you'll do well to seek out those prospects that appreciated your superior concept and understand intellectually what you are advocating.

Too many sales
are lost because
salespeople don't
stay

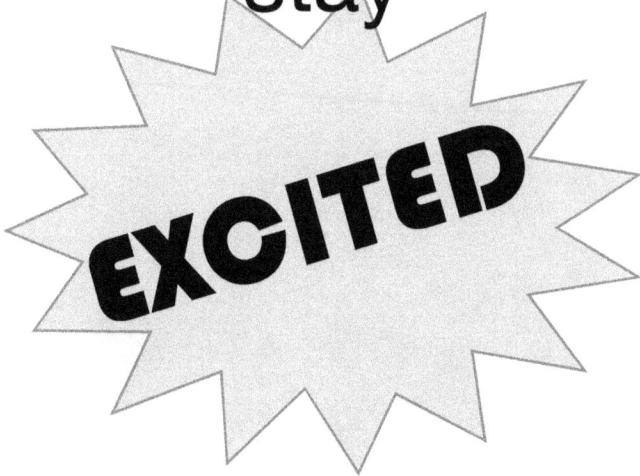

EXCITED

about their product
or service.

Excerpted from *High Energy Sales Thoughts: 101 Positive Sales Thoughts
and Ideas by Carl Henry*

When you stand up *to speak, you sit down richer.*

Hot Tip 8

Power Presenting

Long ago, I figured out a secret that's helped me to earn a lot of money: *When you stand up in front of a group of people, you usually sit down a little richer.* It's simple math. By speaking to many customers at once, you're multiplying your sales efforts because you can sell to more people at the same time. Additionally, you're probably doing a better job than you'd be able to do one-on-one because of the trust that people put in those who aren't afraid to express themselves in public.

The biggest sales I've ever made in my career can be traced back directly or indirectly to my ability to speak in front of a group of people, and I know many salespeople who would say the same thing. When you're talking to a room filled with influencers and decision makers, your sales are bound to skyrocket.

Think speaking in public can't make a big difference in your career? Consider for a moment all of the great men and women who made their mark in history simply by being able to persuade others to see their point of view. I'm not saying that you need to become John F. Kennedy or Martin Luther King, or that your next presentation needs to top the Gettysburg Address in listeners. What I *am* saying, though, is that to neglect this part of your sales repertoire is to turn your back on a massive chance to net new business.

It used to be that only top producers understood the power of public speaking to increase their sales. Over time, however, lots of companies have altered their buying processes to incorporate a 'decision by committee' system. As a consequence, more and more salespeople have improved their presentation skills, to the point that it's less of a competitive edge and more of a survival tactic. Don't let someone else eat your lunch. Become a powerful presenter and see your sales multiply.

So far, we've been talking about the boost in income that you'll see from speaking to groups, but it doesn't end there. Not only will you become richer from the increased sales, but you will become richer as a person. You are doing something that most salespeople, and people in general for that matter, fear. As a result, your confidence will grow and other people will see you as a leader. Like a raise or a promotion, that's the kind of benefit that will probably improve other areas of life, as well.

So what holds so many salespeople back from giving great presentations? I couldn't say for sure, but I'm guessing that stark fear is probably up there. It's often quoted in the media that public speaking is the average person's number one fear. That is, standing up and speaking to a group of customers, friends, or other people is slightly more frightening than death. This is easy to understand. Most of us are naturally shy about expressing our views to everybody and having all the attention on ourselves. What if we sweat, stammer, or say something ridiculous? It's a natural fear to have, and when you fill the room with important prospects, that fear is intensified, because so much is riding on the presentation. If you bomb you may lose more than face. A bad showing might cost you not only the immediate sale, but possibly future sales as well. Plus, no one likes to fail in public.

With that in mind, the first step is to tame your fear. When fighting the nervousness that comes with public speaking, there are really only two things you can do to calm your nerves – practice and be prepared. The practice part is easy. Ideally, I'd just recommend that you give as many presentations as you can to as many people as possible. If you don't have a lot of presenting opportunities, however, or if you'd prefer to start somewhere else, then you could certainly try toastmasters or other practice groups. You could even take an evening or community college course on speaking. While you might not be giving sales presentations in these settings, they can offer a chance to work on your skills in a low-risk setting and increase your confidence.

The other half of the equation, as I mentioned, is preparation. No matter what your speaking talent, you aren't going to do a very good job of convincing anyone to do anything if you don't have any idea of what you're going to say. We'll talk about how you put your presentation together in a moment, but for now, just know that you can't take your preparation lightly.

Of course, for your presentation to be effective, it must be well-delivered. I don't know the exact number of presentations given every day in the world, but I do know that it is in the tens of thousands. I also know, sadly, that most of them are terrible. While presenting is an important sales skill, it isn't one that most of us are born with.

If you are one of the lucky ones who has a knack for speaking and enjoys it, then hone your skills and ride them to the riches. If, however, you're like the rest of us, and could use some help arranging and delivering your presentations, read on. As you'll see, it doesn't have to be difficult. We'll start with Paul Greiner's five minute plan.

Paul Greiner was one of my first bosses. A former math teacher who turned to selling real estate, he was one of my early mentors in the business, especially when it came to presentations. At the time that I knew him, I was giving seminars on real estate in upstate New York. During my first few weeks on the job, I was sent out to speak to a group in a small town. I could tell right away that they were going to be a tough crowd, with their scowls evident through the thick fog of cigarette smoke that sat in the conference room where we met. With a few minutes to prepare, I did what any new salesperson would do – I kept quiet and went about arranging my slides. I figured even if they hated me, I would show them my materials and get out. But then, just before I stepped to the front of the room to begin my presentation, I dropped my slides. As they spilled out onto the floor, so did my confidence and my game plan.

With no other options, I simply got up and winged the presentation. I'm lucky enough to have grown up in Northern New Jersey, just a few miles from New York City. Like any kid in my neighborhood, I could BS my way through a knife fight. Still, the longer I spoke, the less interested my audience seemed. Finally, after an hour, I finished my largely-invented pitch, and the few remaining attendees filtered out of the room.

I decided at that moment that the job wasn't worth it. It had sounded like fun, but getting up and selling at seminars wasn't for me. I called Paul to give him the news. There was a long pause on the phone. Finally, I heard his voice on the other end:

"What time do you start tomorrow?" he asked.

"I'm not. I quit."

"Well, if you weren't quitting, what time would you start tomorrow?"

I thought for a moment. "Nine o'clock in the morning."

"Ok. Pull out a slip of paper. Write down 9:00 a.m."

I did.

"Now what would you say at nine?"

I told him that I would introduce myself and the company.

"Write that down. Now we're at 9:05, what would come next?"

For more than half an hour, Paul walked me through the basics of my presentation, and had me sketch out a plan for the next day. And, even though I was skeptical, I went back. I was surprised to find that most of my fear and apprehension had melted away. No matter what happened with my slides, or with my group, I had a plan to get me through that hour. It turned out to be a good meeting, and I've used that strategy every day since, for more than thirty years.

The thing that I want you to learn from this story is to always have a plan. So many salespeople go into a presentation or a meeting cold turkey. They don't know what they're going to say or how they're going to use their time. Sometimes, they don't even know how much time they have. Instead, they just throw out their sales pitch like a fishing line. That's fine if you're retired and have all day, but not if you need to catch something to eat. Having a written plan, no matter how simple, will force you to exercise some discipline to your time and improve your presentations. The next time you're going to meet with a client, write down a few notes on what you'll say and how much time you have. It's a simple thing to do, and it will keep you on track.

As you gain more experience as a presenter, you'll probably notice that speaking to a group is a totally different scenario than one-on-one selling. By definition, to present is to put on a show. So even though it's just another avenue you can use to convey the value of your products and services, you'll want to be more aware of your audience than you'd need to be with a traditional sales pitch. Specifically, you'll need to hold your customers' attention. With any group of people, there are any number of potential distractions, from cell phones to outside noises and even the members themselves. The easiest way to hold their focus is by being enthusiastic.

Again, this is nothing new. Persuasive personalities have always had the ability to captivate us by sharing their views passionately and appealing to our emotions. From Winston Churchill to Vince Lombardi, the rich tradition of inspiring others has been founded on speaking with conviction. You don't have to be looking to win a World War or the Superbowl to learn from their examples. Simply let your excitement come through. It doesn't matter what you're like when you're not presenting. Once it's your turn to speak, you can't be shy. This is the time to shine; the time to demonstrate to the audience or buying committee that you and your company are different. Great presenters are bright, articulate and extremely motivated, and those are exactly the kind of people that we all like to work with. Be bold, and let your best side come through.

No matter what you read in this book or any other, presenting will likely feel awkward and intimidating to you at first. Keep at it though. Over time, you will become comfortable with it, and most likely, eventually learn to prefer it. Again, it's simple math. I would rather present and sell in front of twenty people than have to visit each one and sell to them separately. Wouldn't you?

Presenting in front of a group is a fear that prevents many good salespeople from becoming superstar salespeople. Their fear often comes from lack of knowledge and experience, but it doesn't have to. The key is confidence, and whether yours is high or low, it's self-sustaining. Presenting is hard to do well until you know you can, but once you realize that it's not so hard, you'll find yourself succeeding in ways you never would have imagined.

" A strong salesperson
will not discount their price
without a very,
very good reason. **"**

If You Want to Make Higher Margins, Stop Giving Them Away

Would you give a stranger on the street thousands of dollars, just because they asked for it? For most of us, the answer is probably no. But the truth is, as salespeople, we give away free money all of the time. How? By cutting into our own prices.

It's a situation that we all know too well. You've met with a potential client, gone through all the wonderful benefits that your product offers, and moved to close the deal. Everything seems perfect until the customer pauses and says something to the effect of: "I'd love to buy from you, but the price is too high."

What's the next move? Too often, it's to offer a slight discount and make the sale. I can understand why most salespeople are so quick to give in on prices. After all, it's easy. The only thing standing between a sale – not to mention the commission that comes with it – is a small concession. Sure, it might mean taking a small hit, but it's better than getting nothing. And, really, what's the big deal?

While it might not seem like anything major at the time, cutting into your margins can really wear down your production, and your career, over the long haul. In fact, it can mean the difference between being a top producer and struggling to make ends meet. Let's take a quick look at the several ways in which discounting can hurt you.

The first problem is obvious: you and your company are making less on the sale than list price. You're giving up some of your profit for nothing. Whatever the standard commission on your particular widget is, you're getting less of it. And it doesn't stop with you. Your employer now has that much less to spend on designing new widgets, handing out bonuses, or booking you a reward trip to Bora Bora. In and of itself, this would be enough of a reason not to cave on price, but it turns out this is only the most minor and immediate effect.

You see, when you discount for customers, you're also putting a cycle of expectation into play. It starts with customers, who, knowing that they can wear you down, will continue to do so. You've set their expectations of price at a new, lower, point. No amount of pleading or arguing is likely to get the price back up to where it should have been. It can only decrease or remain the same. As soon as you've given your ground once, you aren't going to get it back. Make no mistake, it will be very, very difficult to get them back up to full fee. You might not even be able to make another sale to them if you try. Or, more likely, now that the customer has learned that it's easy to wear you down on price, they will continue to do so. If the price started at $100, and they worked you down to $95, then next time they'll probably ask for $90, hoping that you'll give in.

Nor does it end just with the customer that you've given a break. No matter how many times they've promised to keep the special price to themselves, you can be sure that their colleagues and referrals will demand the same treatment and accept nothing less. It's one of those unfortunate truisms in sales: discounts spread like rumors and wildfires.

This might sound a bit harsh. After all, shouldn't you be on the same team with your customers? Isn't there a win-win relationship? There is, but you'll have to work for it. If you really believe in what you're selling, then the customer's win should be the fine performance of what you're offering – at the fair price that you quoted. I'm a big advocate for being invested in your client's success, but this is the one place where your interests are probably not going to be in line. There is a zero-sum negotiation at play.

What you want must come from what they have, and vice-versa.

It's not going to be easy, so be prepared. Customers are masters of manipulation. Each of them has had a lifetime of being a consumer. They all know, more or less, how sales works, and that you have exactly one motivation – to make a sale. By suggesting that the price is too high, they raise a small obstacle to reaching your goal that can be reached by just giving up. After they've raised the issue, the silence and tension that follow can become palpable and unbearable. The whole venture has suddenly been thrown into doubt. *'I have other people who want to sell to me,'* the customer reminds you. *'If you don't give me this, you might not make a sale.'*

The pressure to surrender is hard to handle, but remember what's at stake. Once you've caved, you're probably not going to get another chance at full fee. You've created a long-term problem. A precedent has been set for them, and for their contacts. The customer is going to keep playing the game, because they're better at it than you are.

Perhaps worse than that, however, is that you've set a precedent for yourself. Discounting comes to be a habit, a crutch that we rely on to make sales. The next time someone complains about the price, it's that much easier to give in. It relieved the pressure last time, didn't it? Once it becomes ingrained, you might even start knocking the price down yourself. Having trouble with a tough prospect? Throw him a discount to ease things up. You'll be making less, but it seems like a handy way to avoid the confrontation. Discounting is like any other habit. The more reinforced it becomes, the harder it will be to break.

There are some sales trainers who believe, or at least say, that there is no such thing as a price objection. In their minds, clients have unlimited budgets, and any discussion of price is just a tactic to hide their real reason for not being ready to buy. In the real world, this theory doesn't hold water. Today's market is competitive. People are under more pressure than ever before to get more out of their budgets. They will need to account for what they spend.

Which leads us to the point that strong salespeople recognize and their weaker colleagues miss: Price is always an issue; it's just not the *only* issue or usually even the *most important* one. To succeed in sales, you must realize that price will always matter to your customer, but you shouldn't make it matter more to you than it does to them. They're concerned about it, but probably not as much as they are about the quality of what you're selling, or the service that goes with it. Focus on what you can deliver to justify your prices, not on what you can give away for nothing.

Learning not to give away your margins is straightforward, but that doesn't make it easy. The first step is to practice holding firm. When you meet with new clients, remind yourself beforehand that you aren't going to sacrifice your price. Simply refuse to budge, even if you think it might cost you the sale. Don't mention the possibility of a discount, and if they ask for one, explain that it's not possible and go back into the benefits of what you're selling.

Be careful, though, not to say too much. Silence and confidence are your best friends. By using the wrong wording, you can actually trigger the objection yourself. If you begin the discussion by saying *"Well I normally charge…,'*or *'The standard fee is,'* you're just inviting the customer to balk at what you're asking. Instead, be confident. Use stronger language. Let them know right up front, *"The fee is…,"* or *"The cost is…"* Better yet, frame it in a way that emphasizes the benefits by saying *"The investment is…"* But no matter how you do it, don't create an opening yourself. If the customer wants to try to haggle over price, make them bring it up.

Also, recognize your relative positions in the negotiation. As I said before, clients can put you in a seemingly impossible position by saying that they want to give you what you want – the sale – only after you've given up a bit of your profit. It would seem that the entire burden is on you, but it's not. Even though customers' wants and needs might be more hidden than your own, they're there. They wouldn't be talking to you if they weren't interested in what you're selling. By the time you've gotten around to discussing prices, they've tipped their hand that they'd like to buy. You're now roughly nine-tenths of the way to a sale. All that's left to do is to either hold out – many customers will object to price just to see if they can shake a few extra nickels out of your pocket – or convince them that the benefits of your widgets outweigh the costs. Note that in both cases, the customer wants to buy from you. Practice holding out, and you'll see that you'll be able to make the sale and get your full due. It might hurt at first, but after a while standing firm will become second nature and you won't have to fight the impulse to cave in so easily.

Besides practice, the simplest way to combat price erosion is to have knowledge about your field. Know your product and your competition inside and out, and you'll be better prepared to deal with objections over the cost. How much does your closest competitor charge for the same thing? Do you even have a close competitor, or does not buying from you mean a decrease in quality? What about warranties? The questions you need to ask yourself might differ, but the principle remains the same – the more you know, the easier it will be to show your customers where your value is, and why it should cost what you say it does.

Another good tip is to be busy. We all know that when business isn't so great, confidence can start to get low. Go long enough without new prospects and you could find yourself overly dependent on one or two deals. And as the cupboards go bare, you don't have a lot of leverage to work with. You feel like you'd do *anything* to make a sale and get the cash register moving again. Customers can sense this and take advantage by beating you up on prices. Contrast this with times when prospects are overflowing. When you have more business than you can handle, there's no reason to cut prices. If someone comes in with an offer that is less than you'll get elsewhere, you can take it or leave it. One of the surest ways to sell more, both overall and in terms of higher margins, is to make sure that you're always looking for new business. Build a steady stream of prospects so that you're not dependent on any one deal, and you won't have to offer discounts to keep the new orders coming in.

Finally, know when to cut. At the end of the day, and even after all the reasons I've just given to hold firm to your prices, recognize that there are times when it makes good business sense to give in a little. Maybe you have a leftover or discontinued product that will be worth less in the future than it is now. Perhaps you owe someone a favor. Or, it could be that business *is* really slow and you decide that something is better than nothing.

If you do sacrifice on price, whatever the reason, be sure that the customer knows you're doing it, why you're doing it, and that they shouldn't expect it in the future. Don't give anything away for free. When customers ask for price reduction, they're trying to lower your expectation of what you should be paid. Instead of caving in quickly, lower their expectation of what they'll get. For instance, if they're going to pay less, then you might negotiate faster payments or slower delivery. Or, you could decrease the amount of service that they will receive after the purchase. Regardless of what it is, you should get in the habit of taking away features for reductions in price. Teach your customers that if you're going to give something up, they're going to as well. Employ this strategy well, and you'll receive fewer and fewer objections on price.

The point isn't that you should never, ever discount your prices. The point is that you should have a very, very strong reason for doing so, and that you do it intelligently. There are times when it's better to make a deal at less than your normal price than to get none at all. But make sure they know why you're cutting the price, and by how much you're cutting it. Don't take it as permission to give away the farm and think you're doing a great job. Discounts should be very rare; the exception and not the rule.

We wish that everyone would just pay us what we want, but a good salesperson knows that we have to fight for our price. It's hard to do at first, and even harder after you've gotten used to giving your clients what they want. But, stick with it and you'll find that it will pay off quickly. Beyond the immediate bump in your paycheck, holding firm on your margins might actually help your closing percentage. By showing confidence in your prices and your product, you increase the value in your customer's mind, reinforcing the idea that it's worth what you're asking. Your customers know that value and delivery are more important than price. Remind yourself once in a while, and you'll have an easier time.

People won't buy the

WORST

product from a good salesperson, but will buy a

lesser

product from a great salesperson.

Excerpted from *High Energy Sales Thoughts: 101 Positive Sales Thoughts and Ideas* by Carl Henry

> *If you want to earn* like a million-dollar producer, then you can't afford to be doing five dollar an hour jobs.

To Make Big Money, Stop Working for Minimum Wage

C hances are, you wouldn't be reading this book if you didn't want to earn like a top producer. After all, most of us got into sales to make money. And yet, without thinking about it, many of us do work that pays nearly nothing every day. Why? Because we don't manage our time effectively.

This concept came to me many years ago from my friend and mentor Floyd Wickman. "It's simply impossible," he told me, "to become wealthy by doing minimum wage work." I wasn't exactly blown away. "But most salespeople," he went on to explain, "insist on doing five dollar an hour jobs." His meaning started to dawn on me. Instead of doing the one thing that pays – selling – we get wrapped up in other tasks that would best be dealt out to others or ignored altogether.

What are some five dollar an hour jobs? For starters, typing, filing, cleaning the office, and making very routine phone calls and e-mails are all good candidates. None of them will lead directly to a sale, require your sales skills, or make you a better salesperson. It's not that these things don't have to be done, but that they don't have to be done by you.

Don't confuse being busy with being successful. Wasting time is bad, but working inefficiently can hurt you as much or more in the long run. Some bad habits – hanging out by the water cooler, long coffee breaks, surfing the internet – are easier to break because we know that we shouldn't be doing them in the first place. But with inefficient work, you aren't just shuffling, you're doing something. And that's the worst thing about five dollar jobs, the thing that makes them so deadly; they make you feel like you're busy. And, really, you are. But you aren't doing the things that are going to result in sales. Want an easy way to tell if you're doing five dollar jobs? If you're always busy, but you aren't making much money, guess what? *You are.*

The key to getting the most from your time is to identify and concentrate on sales activities. These include things that you do to make sales, like prospecting, qualifying and closing, as well as those things that help you to be better *at* sales, such as reading sales books, increasing your product knowledge, or ongoing training.

For everything else, you want to do one of three things: delegate, automate, or minimize. Many, if not most, of the five dollar jobs we do can be passed off to someone else. Instead of cleaning your office, pay someone a few dollars a week to do it. Not only will it free you up to do your own work, but it's more efficient as well. A professional cleaner with equipment and experience can get through the job much faster than you could, and do a much better job than you would have anyway. The same thing applies to typing, filing and other non-sales tasks. You'll be much better off spending a few bucks to have it done, than you would be to miss out on time you could use selling.

One of the biggest objections you'll hear about delegating work is that it's expensive. This couldn't be further from the truth. For starters, professional cleaners, filers, typists and the like can all be had for very reasonable fees. If you don't know anyone and can't garner any recommendations from friends or colleagues, then job search and community websites have made it easier than ever to find cheap help in an instant. But, if you're newer in your career or for some other reason can't justify the expense right now, there are still other options. Family members, students, seniors and interns can all be great help for some spare change or a favor. It doesn't matter where you find them, only that they can help with those activities that take you away from your sales work. For a brief amount of up-front training and a small hourly or weekly wage, these people can be a massive help while building up great work experience for themselves. Everybody wins.

Besides, when you take the longer view, the better question isn't whether you can afford help; it's whether you can afford to do these jobs yourself. Think of the last big account you closed, and the commission it brought you. How much time did you spend finding the client, meeting with them, qualifying and closing? Now, think of how much you earned from the sale. Chances are, it adds up to a pretty impressive per-hour sum. Concentrate your efforts on those tasks, and you'll see a big payoff.

Other five dollar jobs can be automated. That is, you can do them once and then repeat them instantly thereafter. A good example of this is e-mail. How many times a week do you send out the same response to a question about one of your product's features or pricing? Don't waste time typing it in again and again. Spend a few minutes, word it as best as you possibly can, and then store it somewhere on your computer. Do this with any type of communication, electronic or otherwise, that you need frequently. Soon, you'll have a file with all your boilerplate answers that you can send to clients in an instant. Since each one can be pasted into an e-mail with only minimal changes, you'll save hours each week and give your customers better thought-out answers.

Finally, for those jobs that just can't be outsourced or automated, find a way to minimize the time you're spending on them. Suppose that every few months you have to order office supplies. Maybe you don't know how many pens, paperclips, and so on you're going to need, so you can't simply place an ongoing order, but that doesn't mean you can't save time. Make a list of what you purchase from time to time. Open an account with one of the big office supply mega stores, and leave a payment method on file. Then, once a month, go online for five minutes and make your order instead of going to the store.

These are just a few examples, but the reality is that almost any five dollar job can be made into less of a time burden. For the next two weeks, keep a log of your work. Just before you leave the office, write down everything you've done at the end of each day, being as complete as possible. After you've done this for a while, go back to the list and the activities that are on it. Look at each one and think about whether or not they're advancing your sales career, and if you'd be better off sending them out to someone else.

Once you do narrow your week down to sales tasks, learn not to obsess on the finer points. Of course, you should always do great work, but don't spend more time than you should on any one thing. Perfectionism can kill your business as fast as sloppy work can. Don't be sloppy, but don't take an hour doing something flawlessly when you could have done it well in ten minutes.

I find a lot of examples of this in my own life. In the course of my work week, I send hundreds of e-mails to the colleagues, clients and prospects that I do business with. I tend to keep my messages short, and after I write out each one, I take a second to look them over. As long as everything seems to say what it should, I hit 'send.' Every once in a while, I'll find that I've made a typo, forgotten a word, or made some other small error that's somehow escaped my less-than-rigorous system. I once had someone ask why I don't do a better job of looking them over before I send them off. My answer? Because I don't get paid to proofread e-mails; I get paid to convey information clearly. Yes, I want to express myself in a way that isn't clumsy or makes me look uneducated, but people understand that electronic messages like e-mail and texts are not held to the same high standard as the State of the Union Address. To look over each character would be counterproductive.

This isn't just my opinion. I have science on my side. In the 1950's, an author named Cyril Northcut Parkinson devised a law that took on his name. The law is this: Work expands to fill the time available for its completion, or more simply, *however many hours you have to do something is how long it will take you.*

Whether you accept this or not at first glance, consider it for a moment. Suppose you have four hours to prepare a client's proposal. You might spend the first hour choosing fonts or a layout, followed by another hour or two of actually typing in the information. To finish it off, you could spend another couple of hours looking for more information, adding graphs, or discussing it with coworkers. Now, imagine that you have half an hour to finish the same proposal. Chances are, you'd put down the main facts and considerations, add a few notes, and then pass it along to an assistant to be finished. Which proposal will be stronger? It's possible that in the first case you'd have included more, but how much of it will be necessary or helpful to the prospect? And what do you think would bring you more sales, a single five hour-proposal, or five completed in the same time?

If you want to make big money, adopt the same mindset with your work. Do your job well, and then let it be. When something is finished, it's finished. Put it away and move on to the next thing. As Peter Drucker pointed out, one of the biggest blunders in business is that "We're more concerned with doing things correctly than doing the right thing."

Most of us don't really value our time as much as we should. Think about things this way. If you're going to make $100,000 a year, assuming that you're going to take a couple of weeks of vacation each year, then you're going to have to earn $2,000 a week, or around $50 per hour if you're working a solid forty a week. Where is that $50 going to come from? The numbers get even more compelling if you've set your sights higher. Set your sights on a lofty quarter of a million, and you need to be making $125 an hour. Still think spending three hours rearranging your desk is a good idea?

As your sales career progresses, you should be working to do more selling and less of everything else. Find a way to remove tasks that aren't helping you to sell, and learn to do good work without being a perfectionist. Over time, those extra hours spent prospecting and closing will pay you back with a much higher income.

Something to Think About

A customer once asked me,

Do you work on Saturday?

I replied...

Do you buy on Saturday?

Excerpted from *High Energy Sales Thoughts: 101 Positive Sales Thoughts and Ideas* by Carl Henry

"Teachers are all around us.

If you listen carefully and observe closely

they will show you

the secrets of their success."

The Teachings of Kaszubinski and Others

I have always been a student. In the years since I've left school, I've never stopped learning, and I've never been ashamed to admit I learned something from someone else. Because of this attitude, I've been able to pick up skills and techniques that never would have come to me otherwise.

I've found that amongst successful salespeople, this is not unusual. Nearly every top performer I've met has told me the same thing – they've taken important lessons from friends and colleagues and incorporated them into their own careers. In this chapter you'll learn some of the secrets I've gathered from others over the years.

Ken Kaszubinski

Let me start by telling you about my friend Ken Kaszubinski who inspired me to write this chapter. I've known Ken for over eighteen years, dating back to the beginning of his sales career. He attended a sales seminar that I presented for his company. After my seminar, Ken took the tools he'd learned and applied them tirelessly to his work. In a short time, he went from the bottom of the charts to breaking company sales records. Soon after, he was promoted into management, where he's gone out to turn several of his company's poorest-performing regions into top moneymakers.

The first thing to realize about Ken is that he simply flat-out works harder than anyone I know. There's just no substitute for the willingness to get the job done no matter what it takes. I truly believe that he was destined to succeed in sales for that reason alone.

However, there are two other things that I've learned from watching Ken over the years that I think are important to take from his success.

First, he's never afraid to make a decision. If he sets a goal, he decides what needs to be done and does it. There is no waffling, no long meetings, and no going back and forth. He taught me that it's better to find the best choice and make it. Don't hold back.

Another great thing Ken taught me was the value of *everyday sales*. Every salesperson wants to make the big close – the giant account that makes their year and means a huge bump in income and prestige. Those sales are great, and nothing compares to the feeling of having one come through. The problem is, they tend to come few and far between. And while you're waiting for those big accounts to hit, you could be building your career through smaller sales. These every day sales are the kind that won't make you a hero, but will keep you making new contacts, working on your skills, and paying the bills. Cultivate a steady stream of these smaller accounts, and you won't have so much pressure to sell something big.

It's important to point out that every day sales aren't always actual orders. You might work in an industry where there aren't any small sales – industrial manufacturing, commercial real estate, and so on. The point isn't that you have to close on something each day, but that you set small goals that get you closer. So, if you can't realistically make a string of small sales, do what you can to keep the phone ringing and your sales funnel full. Don't wait for your dream sale to come in, keep at it and make your own luck.

Russ Atkinson

In the eighties, an economist named Arthur Laffer made big news by changing the way policy makers viewed taxes and revenues. Drawing on some older ideas, he showed how charging people less in taxes might mean more for the government, the idea being that citizens might earn more and thus pay larger amounts despite the smaller percentages. To illustrate his point, he sketched a quick diagram on a napkin that became known as the 'Laffer Curve.'

Because this is a book on sales and not economics, I'm not concerned with whether or not you agree with Laffer or not. Either way, he had hit upon an important point: sometimes less is more, and vice versa. How does this apply to sales and you?

A great friend of mine, Russ Atkinson, happened upon the Laffer Curve one day, and noticed that there was a similarity between the economic concept being shown, and the day-to-day life of a salesperson. As a sharp sales manager, he noticed that each time one of his reps would make a big sale, their commissions would decrease in the following weeks and months. How could this be? Why should they make a big sale, only to see their production decrease again immediately?

The answer was simple and obvious. As salespeople, the kinds of things we do to drum-up business

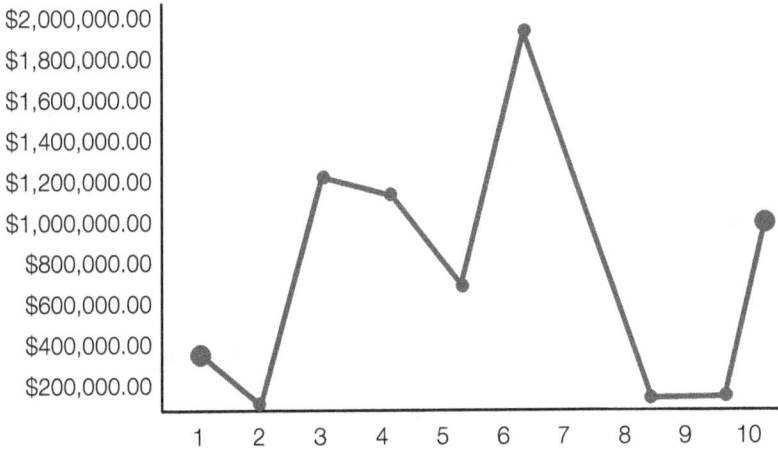

A graph of Russ's sales team over the course of ten months. Notice the up-and-down pattern.

– prospecting, meeting new clients, asking for referrals – are exactly what we stop doing once we have a strong lead or an imminent sale. In other words, we take our eyes off the horizon and look at what's directly in front of us.

After recognizing the trend, Russ took steps to fix it. He taught his sales force that making a big sale was great, but that prospecting and looking for new business are things that they have to be doing all the time. It's easy to get caught up in the excitement of a big sale, but where will you be afterwards? The choice is yours. You can either keep looking for business and have a pipeline full of leads, or start again at square one after each big sale. Where would you rather be?

Jim Kerr

How would you like a single, easy-to-use tip that could boost your income right away? You're in luck, because that's exactly the sort of tip I got from Jim Kerr. When I met Jim, he was already a very successful salesperson in the machine tool industry. Not only was he the standard by which his firm measured production, but he was loved by his customers as well. One morning, I met Jim for a cup of coffee to talk about his methods. He boiled his success down to one thing: *A clean piece of paper.*

You might be wondering how a blank sheet can magnify your sales potential. The secret is in human nature. You see, as salespeople, we all have a tendency to skip steps. We learn our products and our benefits so well, that we start to imagine that they are the answer to every problem, before we've even thought the customer's situation through. I can speak to this from personal experience. Over the years, I've had wonderful success with my MODERN Selling System. Not only has it worked for me, but I've passed it along to thousands more in talks and seminars, who have in turn found it to be helpful. But as fantastic as it is, I've noticed that in my mind, it seems like a perfect solution to almost every problem:

Carl, I need more leads.

My MODERN Selling System is a perfect answer.

Carl, I have a headache.

I'm glad you brought it up. You should try my MOD-ERN Selling System.

Of course, I'm being a bit ridiculous, but the point is that we're all inclined to see our own products as solutions for others. Our customers, however, usually don't see things the same way, and will resent a salesperson who they feel doesn't understand their problems. That's where the clean sheet comes in. The next time you're with a prospect or customer, take one out. Start at the beginning, and go over their needs one piece at a time. Ask questions and take careful notes. Give them the time to tell you what they need, and be sure not to assume anything. By taking out a clean sheet of paper, you don't skip steps in the sales process or get ahead of yourself. It also shows the customer that you care, and forces you to find out their real needs before you present a solution. Do that consistently, and you'll find that your sales will sky-rocket. It's easy; just remember that every customer deserves a clean sheet of paper.

William T. Brooks

Bill was one of the first people that I met in the speaking and seminar industry, and I began to look up to him almost immediately. I'd had some great success in sales, and was just beginning to make a name for myself as a trainer when we met. I had just moved to North Carolina and was having a hard time adjusting to my new career and surroundings. I met Bill at a conference, where he took the time to talk with me about my work and where I wanted to go in life. I took his advice very seriously, and we stayed in touch. As a fellow salesperson and New Jersey native who was a few years older than I was, he seemed a natural fit for a mentor.

From there, Bill helped guide me into the business. Not only did he show me the basics of effective presentations, but he also embodied all of the qualities that I was trying to instill in my programs – making selling a profession instead of a job, developing client relationships, and having fun with what you do. He understood all of these concepts and was living them at a higher level than I was.

Over the years, I continued to talk with Bill from time to time. He taught me to seek out those people who are doing what you want to do. Don't imitate them, but emulate them. The idea isn't to be a clone of someone else, but to utilize their experience in your own work. Take the time to locate a mentor and ask them 'Am I going in the right direction?' There is almost nothing in this world that isn't made easier by having the help of someone who's farther along the road than you are. Find them, and don't be afraid to ask for directions. If you associate with top producers and leaders you will be more successful.

John McDonald

John was a sales manager for a large, international manufacturer that I worked with for several years. He once gave me a simple tip that has served me well. Early in our relationship, we had been discussing a training session and I'd called to confirm a detail. In leaving him a message on his voicemail, I spoke so quickly that he couldn't make out my number. In order to get it, he had to replay the voicemail several times. Eventually, he was able to return my call, but he could have just as easily deleted the message and moved on. When he mentioned his trouble, and asked me to slow down next time, it hit me like a bolt of lightning. Here was a great client, and by rushing through my calls, I was making it hard for him to do business with me. How many sales had I lost because customers couldn't hear how to reach me? The point here is simple: slow down when giving your phone number and contact information. Speak more slowly than you think you need to. If you don't, it could cost you a sale.

Tom Reilly

Tom is one of my best friends in the speaking and training business. He is the guy who wrote the first sales books on value-added selling. The premise of value added selling is simple: you should set your prices at a point that is fair for both you and your customer, and then stick to them.

When a customer says that your price is too high, it's easy to offer a discount to close the deal. In the short run, this might seem like a winning strategy, but it's likely to cost you over time. Why? Because you're essentially telling your customers that you agree with them – your price is too high. A better track is to explain the value of your work, or help the customer find a way to bring in the money from elsewhere. It might be tougher at first, but in the long run you'll get less resistance by staying firm with your prices. I would suggest that you add Tom Reilly's books to your personal sales library.

Floyd Wickman

Over two decades ago, Floyd taught me how to create urgency in a customer's mind. He called it the takeaway close. Pick up any basic psychology text-book and you'll see something interesting: the fear of loss is a greater motivator than the opportunity to gain. Think about your own life. Have you every no-ticed that when you don't need a sale you are a better salesperson, a better negotiator? The same principle works on the other side of the table. When customers know you are busy they want you even more.

The takeaway close, which relies on this basic human instinct, is easy to learn and very powerful, psychologically. It relies on the simple human desire to associate with successful people. For instance, suppose a customer calls to schedule an appoint-ment with you. You know that your calendar is clear, but rather than appear to be overly eager, you simply respond, "Let me check my schedule and get back with you shortly." Don't call to confirm the appoint-ment right away, create a bit of anticipation. When a reasonable amount of time has passed, maybe a couple of hours, you agree to the meeting, noting that you were "able to move some things." I should point out that you don't have to lie to your custom-ers. Just shape the facts to give the impression that you're busy and successful. After all, they don't have to know that the meeting you bumped was with your dog in the park.

Remember that customers want to buy from suc-cessful people. If you give the impression that you've got nothing to do, your clients will treat you accordingly. On the other hand, if they feel that you are a busy professional, they will have more respect for your time and attention.

Keith Carlisle

Keith was another young salesperson who attended one of my sale seminars and ran with the concepts he learned. Before he found his way into sales, Keith had been competitive in martial arts. On the surface, these might seem like entirely different fields. However, he soon found that the principles he'd studied to fight weren't all that different from what it took to succeed in his new profession. I caught up with him recently, when he explained his success and told me about something he liked to call 'Secretarial Kung Fu.'

Watch any old kung fu movie, and you'll come upon a scene where two masters square off in battle. Relying on their years of skill and precision, they will circle each other with great respect, looking for even the slightest positional advantage. Once one feels that they've gained the upper hand, an attack will commence and the battle will play out honing each other's skills. At its core, the ancient martial art is more about position and focus than it is punches and kicks. But what does this have to do with sales?

Secretaries and salespeople, Keith explained, are natural adversaries. Like the kung fu masters from the movies, they've developed relative specialties – one side works at getting to decision makers, while the other is an expert at keeping people from them. Put another way, the salesperson desperately wants into the temple, while the assistant will fight to the death to keep them out.

And, just as in the movies, only careful practice and preparation will get you past the gatekeeper. Sharpen your skills, recognize that your opponent is only doing their job, learn from every encounter and you just might find your way through those doors.

Dr. Donald Lord

Dr. Lord was a surgeon in Ridgewood, New Jersey. His lifelong love of learning had led him through not only a brilliant medical career, but also a strong track record of real estate investments. His first few investments, started on a shoestring before World War II, had blossomed into millions in the seventies.

As a young real estate broker, I'd heard through the grapevine that he was planning on renting a small carriage house on his large farm estate. Hoping to find a good home in an upscale neighborhood, I decided to pay Dr. Lord a visit. When I found him, he wasn't looking over balance sheets or calling CPA's. Instead, he was out on his property painting one of his barns and enjoying the sun. After a short conversation, we agreed that I would rent the carriage house.

After my wife and I moved in, we slowly became part of the family. Because our home was on the estate, we ran into Dr. Lord frequently. He was never anything but generous with his advice and attention. Over time, I learned the secret of his success: thinking bigger.

No matter what my goal or idea, he would always encourage me to think bigger, to want more out of my life. As a man who had become wealthy beyond his hopes, he understood what's out there in the world for each of us, if we just set our minds to it.

Seek out someone who has been wildly successful, whether it's in sales or another field. Spend time with them and think about the scope of their goals. Are you dreaming in the same league? If not, learn to think bigger. Learn to stretch further in your imagination, and you'll be surprised at what you can reach.

Rich Marino

Have you ever talked your customer right out of a sale? Business executive Rich Marino calls this the 'dump truck routine.' Once a salesperson finds a prospect, they dump feature after feature on them without stopping to gauge a reaction. When the time to close comes, the salesperson is still too busy throwing out features to notice. Eventually, the customer starts to have new questions and concerns and decides to do more research before buying. Remember, don't sell with a *blah*, *blah*, *blah*, when a single *blah* will do.

Elsie Faes

Elsie is one of the most successful brokers I've ever met, for one simple reason – she qualifies like it's an Olympic sport. I used to love to watch her sell real estate. Day after day, she would bring in a new batch of couples eager to hit the pavement and see some homes. But before she would show them a single home, she would sit them down and patiently go over their needs and budget. Sometimes this would take hours or even days, but then a miraculous thing would happen: more often than not, her buyers would make an offer on one of the first three houses she showed them. Instead of driving around to dozens of homes for weeks on end, she had simply learned to find out exactly what a homebuyer wanted and then show it to them. Learn from her example and find out everything you can about your customer's needs. Not only will you sell more, but you'll save yourself a lot of time, too.

Al Miller

If you don't get excited about your product, how can your customer? That's what I learned from Al Miller, then president of a machinery company I used to work with. He told me a story that's stuck with me for years. A customer was in the showroom, looking at a machine Al's company sold. A salesperson greeted him, found out about his needs, and went through a product demo. Everything was professional and well-rehearsed, but the customer didn't buy. Al didn't think anything of it, until he found out a few days later that the man had bought from a competitor. Al had done business with this customer before, so he decided to call him on the phone and ask why he'd chosen a different firm's product. His answer was surprising. "Your salesperson just didn't seem excited by your machine."

Al learned what we all know intuitively – that excitement is contagious, and so is boredom. Be proud of what you sell and be enthusiastic in your work. Everyone has good days and bad, but try to leave personal issues and past failures behind. Customers can sense how you feel and will pick up on your lead. Show some excitement and you just might get something to be excited about.

Steve Akley

My client and friend Steve Akley passed along to me a tip that has helped him to break the ice with his clients and prospects. Whenever he finds himself with a person or group he doesn't know, he simply asks them to tell him something interesting about themselves.

It's amazing how such a simple question can yield big results. By going beyond the obvious – education, experience, etc. – that everyone asks about, he's able to force the other person to think about their response and engage him in a meaningful way. Plus, he often hears something that he wouldn't have expected. In the few years since he started, Steve tells me that he's heard about how one client had been a female guard in an all-male prison, how another competes in a roller derby in her spare time, and how a third used to be a bail bondsman. He has dozens more, but the real benefit isn't in the stories, interesting and entertaining as they may be. Through this easy way to take the conversation away from standard business-talk, he gets to know his clients and prospects in a way that he otherwise wouldn't.

Take a few minutes to ask some open-ended questions of your clients. It will let you get to know them a little better, and you might just get a great story out of it.

David Schwartz

Want to sell more? Then get out of your comfort zone. It's human nature to return to the spot where we've hit pay dirt before. This is especially true for salespeople. Just as an old fisherman will always return to the hole where he caught 'the big one,' we have an innate urge to keep prospecting the same places in the same way. There's nothing wrong with keeping wraps on your best customers and prospects, but don't get stuck there. Break out and try some new areas. You might find a new favorite spot.

Don & Matt Terrace

Don and Matt Terrace were two of my earliest employers. They were both great guys, and strong believers in continuous training. Rather than send their sales staff off to a seminar once or twice a year, they drilled us like we were going to war. Like drill sergeants, they hit us each morning with mental push-ups – sample cold calls, customer objections and trial closes. Every day was a chance to learn and practice. They imprinted on us the idea that effective sales required constant learning and preparation, an idea that I've passed on to thousands since.

Spend your time finding out who has the power to make a decision before you

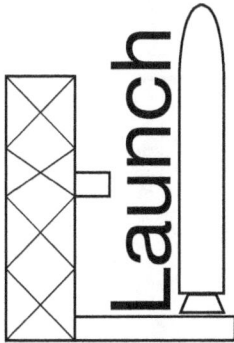

Launch

into a presentation.

Excerpted from *High Energy Sales Thoughts: 101 Positive Sales Thoughts and Ideas* by Carl Henry

"If you aren't reading sales books, *you're probably **being outsold** by someone who is.*"

Building Your Personal Sales Library

When I'm in the middle of one of my seminars, I like to pose a question to the audience. Usually, I'll ask who in the room takes their job seriously. Always, the hands shoot up. Then, I'll pick someone with their hand raised, and ask the name of the last sales book they read. Nine times out of ten, they're silent. I'll move on to the next person; what was the last book they read to help their career? Again, more often than not, they can't name one. This continues for a bit until, invariably, it becomes apparent that very few of my attendees have read anything in the past five years that might help them sell more.

I point this out not to denigrate my seminar attendees, but to point out that most of us aren't taking our careers seriously enough. Think about it for a moment; can you imagine people failing to read in any other occupation? Most of us want to be paid like lawyers or surgeons, but would we hire one of either that wasn't continually trying to get better at what they do, or at least keeping up on their industry?

Worse still are the sales managers who have never read any books on selling or management. Think of all that's been learned and written about presenting, time management, and goal-setting. How can anyone be prepared to lead and manage others without having at least a passing interest and background on these topics?

Reading a book is one of the cheapest sales educations you can get. For a few dollars, you get an expert. He's taken all his knowledge, all his research and experience, and distilled it down into a couple handfuls of pages. He's spent many years, maybe a lifetime, figuring it out, and all you have to do is spend a few hours reading it.

Sales isn't just about putting up decent numbers and making a living. It's also about working smarter, not harder. It's human nature to find a system that works for you and keep repeating it again and again. The problem is, what's worked for us in the past might not be the most efficient way; we become slaves to old habits, when new ones would serve us much better. Many producers, even highly successful ones, work so hard to get one sale, when, if they adapted their approach to work more efficiently, they could have gotten three in the same amount of time.

Once, after a seminar, a few attendees were talking to me about what they'd learned, and a man who'd been there broke down in tears. Startled, I asked him why he was crying. What could I possibly have said about sales that would affect him emotionally? He replied that this was his last seminar; he was due to retire in a month. I congratulated him, but still felt puzzled as to what could have bothered him so much. He explained that, had he known what I had shown him that day, he would have retired ten years earlier. While that's a ringing endorsement, I wondered why he hadn't just gone out and picked up a sales book? It might not have been the same as attending a seminar, but he could have picked up some of the same tools by spending a few quality hours with some sales volumes. Books are just another part of the ongoing training and education that every sales professional should be going through all the time.

Want a simple program that will change your life? Go out to a bookstore on January 1. Or, if the first day of the year isn't coming around anytime soon, pick another day that is. Look for 12 sales books that you think could help you produce more in your career. Read one each month. If you're anywhere near the normal range of reading adults, this won't take you more than a few minutes a day. At the end of the month, put down the finished book and make three or four notes on things you've learned – or relearned – that could help you sell more and make more money.

Better yet, share the books with your colleagues. Pass them around the group, each of you reading something different each month. Then, with a cup of coffee at a morning meeting, or over a drink after work, talk about what you came away with from the month's reading. It doesn't have to be anything elaborate, just a sense of what you could utilize to become more successful.

Recently, I did a two-day seminar for one of my clients. The audience was full of high income, high performing producers. Despite this, when I asked how many of them regularly read sales books, no hands shot up. At the end of the first day, I divided the thirty attendees into two groups. I gave the first half copies of one sales book, and the second half copies of another. I then asked each person to read a different chapter within their book, write down a couple of notes on an index card, and share a thought with the group the next morning.

When the next day came, it was hard to get them settled in to start training. Everyone wanted to talk about the chapter they'd read! By the time they'd finished sharing their notes, every one of them had learned something extra that would help them make more money. If a group of men and women that were already top producers could get so much out of a single chapter, imagine what you could get from a book each month!

You shouldn't only be reading sales books, either. There are a lot of topics that relate to sales indirectly that can assist your understanding of your clients and your career – books on marketing, presenting, psychology, motivation, or even the history of your industry can be helpful. My book *The PEOPLE Approach to Customer Service*, is a good example. As long as you stay within the right topics, there's a good chance that you can learn something that will help you increase your production in the future. Start with sales, but don't be afraid to branch out into other areas that might help out your career as well.

And while we're at it, don't just read books. No matter what you're selling, there are things going on in your business that you should know about. Keep up with the news. Read industry journals or websites. It only takes a few minutes a day, but by staying informed, you'll be better prepared to work with others – inside your own company and out.

As you read, don't be afraid to get involved with your books. Highlight sections, fold page corners, or make notes in the margins. That way, if you pick up the book again at a later time, you won't have to reread the whole thing. All you'll need to do is take a quick look through and make the ideas fresh in your mind again. Too many of us who are reading regularly forget this crucial step. Reading to increase your production is great, but you need to use the information and come back to it once in a while to really retain it. Otherwise, it amounts to nothing more than a short-term boost and some wasted time. It's no different than a golf or tennis lesson. Without lots of practice and a refresher now and then, you're not going to get better very quickly.

Periodically, I run across someone who says that they would read more, but they don't know which ones to buy. How should you know what to read? In the beginning, choosing what to pick up is easy. You can simply peruse your local bookstore or look online for bestsellers in sales. (Personally, I recommend anything by Carl Henry.) You're not likely to find many that aren't helpful out of the titles that millions of salespeople before you have chosen. If you've exhausted those lists, you can try asking other successful salespeople what they're reading. Or, if even that seems like too much trouble, e-mail me and I'll send you a good list to get started.

A lack of time is not an excuse, either. Usually, when people say that they don't have the time to read, what they mean is that they'd rather watch television or have a few beers with their friends. When you really think about it, we're rarely actually 'too busy' to do almost anything that we claim we can't. This is es-

pecially true when it comes to reading, which like getting exercise or eating broccoli, is something that we
all claim to know we need to do more of, but hardly
ever get around to doing. Luckily, for reading there
is a fix that doesn't require eating sprouts or illegal
diet pills. If you really can't, or won't, spare the time
to read a book, then you can listen to one. Between
CD's, mp3's and other formats, a great sales education is never further away than a pair of headphones.

With all of this being said, keep in mind that reading
is only half the effort that's required. Knowing what to
do doesn't absolve you of the responsibility to do it.
I know a salesperson, wickedly smart, who has been
a lifelong reader. Put a book in front of him, and in no
time he'll be able to tell you what the author's point
was, not to mention eight or nine other opinions on
the subject. He could tell you, eloquently and in great
depth, dozens of ways to improve your selling career.
He's brilliant, but he's also a failure. You see, he's only
doing some of the right things. Learning is necessary
and important, but sooner or later you need to go
out and try something. Taking in new techniques and
ideas isn't enough. To profit from them, you have to
go out and sell something. My friend is broke because
he's reading, not doing.

You might not have to wait long. I can recall an
occasion when my friend Bill Brooks sent me over a
draft of his latest book. Always eager to see what he's

come up with, I took in most of it on a short flight. The bulk of his writing was on how to sell at a higher margin than your competition. Basically, it was a step-by-step guide on how to handle things when a client asks you for a reduction in your price. Upon landing, I stashed it into my briefcase and went on my way.

Not five minutes after I'd arrived at my destination terminal, my cell phone rang. The call was from a prospective client that I'd been working with for weeks. He'd love to hire me, he admitted, but wanted to know what I'd offer for a discount. With a small grin, I looked down toward my bag. This poor, unsuspecting client had no idea that I'd just earned my brown belt in negotiation. Using the methods I'd gotten only minutes before, I talked him to full fee and earned myself thousands of dollars that I would have almost certainly lost without the information. Books can have an immediate impact.

Reading isn't just for kids. Obviously, if you're holding this, then you are taking a step in the right direction, but don't let this be the last sales book you ever read. Treat your career seriously, and expose yourself to new ideas that will help you sell more efficiently. It's better to find out what you've been missing now than to have something to cry about later.

Something to Think About

Everyone in your organization

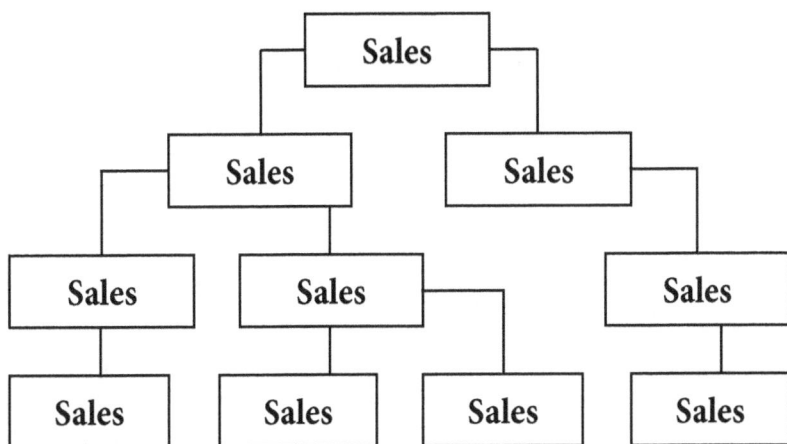

Sales

| Sales | | Sales |

| Sales | | Sales | | | Sales |

| Sales | | Sales | | Sales | | Sales |

can help you sell. Be sure to treat them accordingly.

Excerpted from *High Energy Sales Thoughts: 101 Positive Sales Thoughts and Ideas by Carl Henry*

"Sales is not a single department.

It's everyone's job.

If there are no sales, then nothing else

in a company will matter. "

Developing a Sales Culture

Where are the people in your organization who are responsible for selling? If you answered something like 'in the bullpen,' 'corner office,' or 'the third floor,' then you're probably missing out by not having a sales focused company.

You may notice that throughout this book, I've made a big deal out of the fact that sales is the only department in a company that brings in money. This is for two reasons: because it's true, and it's important. After all, without an effective sales department, there would be no other departments, no other jobs.

Smart companies are capitalizing on this basic fact and integrating a sales focus into every corner of their enterprise. You've probably heard of a sales focus before, but what does it really mean? Very simply, that every single person in your organization is responsible for sales. Of course, account reps and sales managers will be the direct contacts, but each person is aware that reaching out to customers is the lifeblood of the business and does his or her part in contributing to it.

Think of how many people there are in your organization who can hinder or help your sale with their actions. A development team that can provide you with a more competitive product; human resources can hire and bring in the right sort of help and support by looking for candidates that are sales-minded; receptionists can set the proper tone by meeting visitors, whether in person or over the phone, with a tone that invites business; customer service reps can go a long way toward generating repeat sales, or discouraging long-term clients, in the way that they answer questions and address your existing client base; even the janitorial staff can make a difference, by preparing your office for client visits. At every link in the chain is the opportunity to either move a sale along, or become a stumbling block to it.

And, of course, it doesn't just stop with external customers. Different departments can do a lot to help you out on the back end, as well. By working with you on terms and margins, keeping you informed of product and industry developments, getting you better support materials, or pitching in a thousand other ways, non-sales personnel can have a big impact on your production.

Most people in business seem to intuitively understand the benefits of training all of these departments to assist in selling. And yet, in many organizations, there are a number of walls – physically and ideologically – between the producers and 'everyone else.'

That's the opposite of a sales culture, and one that isn't going to help anyone's bottom line. Still, it's not that uncommon. A few years back, I sent along to my clients and friends an article on developing a sales culture along with my electronic newsletter. The response that I received was overwhelming. Clearly, I'd struck a chord with my readers. Almost right away, they stated that the sales culture was lacking at their firms, or they wanted to know what they could do. One after another, the replies came in from those in my address book who felt their organizations could benefit from more wisdom in this area. And that was only the first wave. For more than a year, the topic would return when acquaintances would ask me to send the article again. Why should firms have such a hard time integrating a sales focused approach?

The most obvious reason is a lack of information or perspective. Most people who aren't in sales simply view it as 'someone else's job.' They fail to make the connection between their own interactions with customers or sales staff and the company's bottom line. A bigger problem is when other sections of the company *don't want* to help with sales. Why, you ask, wouldn't they want to help?

Until now, I've been focusing on other departments, but look within your own as well. While it's true that sales is the most important piece of a company, it's not the only one that matters. This a significant piece of information, but one that's too often overlooked by those on the selling end of the stick. I've seen salespeople ruin any chance of cooperation with other departments because they were too arrogant or condescending to anyone who doesn't cold call for a living. This is a serious personality defect, and one that turns out to be expensive. Remember, you're all part of the same team. If you come off as egotistical or demanding, then no one is going to want to help you. And if no one wants to help you, then you're going to have a much harder time getting anything done.

Really, it's all about communication. Do what you can to keep up with your co-workers in other departments. Pass along articles or e-mails that might help. Invite people in to see you. Bring donuts, take them out to lunch. In short, you should make a point of treating co-workers like customers. Be sure that they know what you do, and how you do it. Is there something that you could use to close more business? Then ask for it.

Also, realize that the door swings both ways.

Just as you want these people to take care of you, be sure to take care of them. Close a huge sale with help from the engineering department? Then say so with a gift or a written thank you. Be generous with your applause. Let those who have helped you know that they're contributing to your success. Not only will they appreciate the gesture, they'll want to keep helping you in the future.

If you feel like the sales atmosphere in your firm is a bit lacking, propose something higher up the food chain. As important as it is on a personal level, the whole thing works much better as a top-down approach. Your CEO or Vice President of Sales can probably do more to affect the sales culture of your company in a day than you can in several months. Targeted training to raise awareness of sales as an organization-wide concern is a good first step. Tying production goals to the business as a whole, rather than just the sales department, is another. By giving everyone – from the lowest rung on the ladder to the highest – a vested interest in helping sales to increase, managers make it much more likely that everyone will participate.

Successfully instilling a sales mindset throughout an organization can pay huge dividends – and not just to salespeople. Work to get others in your company involved in raising production, and you could all see a bump in your next paycheck.

> ***Creating lasting value***
> *for your customers*
> *is the surest way to make a sales job*
> *much easier and more profitable.*

Create Lasting Value
for Your Customers

If you watch a decent amount of television, you may have noticed something about advertisements lately. Truck companies, it seems, have figured out a remarkable thing: one of the easiest ways to sell more trucks is by showing old ones working alongside new ones. On the surface, this doesn't make a lot of sense. After all, they aren't making the older models any more, and they wouldn't stand to profit if you bought a used one. So, why all the shots of older trucks hauling mounds of steel and impossibly large logs?

The answer, of course, is that they're selling reliability. By showing, or at least suggesting, that so many of their products are still performing well after decades of hard use, they can speak volumes about quality. This is not at all a revolutionary concept. In fact, it's really a form of the oldest brand of advertising that there is: word of mouth and satisfied customers. There's no better marketing piece than a whole bunch of people who are happily using your products and willing to talk about it. You don't need a multi-million dollar ad agency to make this same concept work for you. All you have to do is build lasting value for your clients.

How do you build value? Like most other things, it's just a matter of being willing to do a bit more work. It all starts with qualifying your prospects the right way. When you're trying to determine their needs, think past making the sale. What will help them out the most in the long run? The answer might not come quickly, but be patient. Ask more questions, and pay close attention to the answers. Look deeper into their problems and think a bit longer about their concerns and objections. By spending this small bit of extra time, you'll set yourself up for a much easier relationship down the road. So go the extra mile to get it done for your customers. Help them make the best choices for their businesses and understand their options. As an added bonus, it will probably save you lots of time in the closing phase. When your clients feel that you have taken the time to understand their needs, they're less apt to throw up objections to the deal.

Once you've made the sale, building value is all

about service. You simply do something that many salespeople won't – treat your clients like prospects. During the build up to the close, you were probably on your best behavior. Stay there. One of the most common complaints about even the greatest salespeople is that they're wonderful and helpful, right up until the moment the sale is made. Then, once the commission has been secured, it's no more roses and candies. I can understand the urge salespeople feel to forget about existing clients. Once we've made the sale, it seems like the battle is over. We've gotten what we wanted. Mentally, we've moved on to the next challenge and are looking for the next commission. It's only natural, and we wouldn't be good at our jobs if we weren't thinking ahead. But for the customer, the relationship is just beginning. They've already invested their money in what you're selling, now they have to use it and live with it. Stay in touch. Send an e-mail or make a quick phone call from time to time. Ask them how business is going, or if their product is working out. Let them know that you want them to be successful. Try to help them get the most out of what you helped convince them to buy. It usually won't take much time, and your clients will be grateful.

Or, if their appreciation isn't sufficient enough motivation for you, then think of the first day after the sale as the beginning of the next one. No sale is ever the last one, and you have the chance to add a prospect for more sales in the future. Even coffin salespeople get repeat business, albeit usually from friends and relatives. Take care of the clients you have, and you'll have an easier time in the future.

If you've qualified properly, the follow-up will normally be pretty simple anyway. Most of the time, when existing customers are dissatisfied or taking up large chunks of our day it's because we either haven't sold them on the right product, told them what to expect, or fully explained things like ongoing costs, maintenance and so on.

It really boils down to the business equivalent of the golden rule. Think of things that you've purchased in your own life. Cars and trucks are obvious examples, but so are homes, computers and electronics. When did you last buy one of these products? Was the salesperson helpful? Were they still as helpful after you'd offered your credit card or signed on the dotted line? And what about what you bought? Is it still serving you well, or do you wish you'd made a different choice? Put yourself in your client's place and ask yourself the same questions. The answers that come to mind will tell you if you're building enough value for them.

Creating lasting value for your customers might seem like more work for you, but as I said in the beginning of the chapter, it's one of the easiest and surest ways to a more profitable sales career. This is because it builds - trust, the one thing that can make a sale very easy, or virtually impossible. Customers have bought from salespeople before; they know that what's promised will not always be delivered, that expectations are not always met. They know that you get paid to sell, and that there is the possibility that if they do business with you, they will be sorry for it later.

All of this is working against you as you move from the first call up to the close. But once you've made it that far, you have an opportunity to turn the tables. By showing that you will do as you've promised or go the extra mile a few times, you can break through that layer of distrust and make it work for you. Now, you're a trusted resource for your contact and their firm. What you say is taken and considered carefully, while salespeople from competing firms are kept at arm's length. Instead of being seen as an outsider who wants to make money, you become a partner who has answers to specific problems.

At this point, some very good things happen for you. The first is that you will get more orders, and for larger amounts. People like to work with others that they trust to deliver. Trying new people and products is always a possibility, but the biggest chunk of business doesn't go to someone who is unknown. Show that you're worthy of their business, and customers will reward you by throwing the lion's share your way.

I can personally attest to this. Some of my clients have been hiring me to train their sales personnel for decades. In some cases, the original contacts have retired and the new managers – originally trainees in my seminars – have retained my services. Others have passed my name along to colleagues and contacts within their industries. I have one company that I work with that has passed from father to son, and I've kept training for them all the while. That kind of loyalty doesn't happen by accident. At every seminar, and for every group, I try to give one hundred and ten percent. I never want to let down anyone who's hired me, and they've rewarded me by bringing me back again and again. Because of this, I rarely have to do any sort of marketing. I've generated enough goodwill that work keeps coming in. Better yet, for the most part, they know that my programs are going to be worth it and don't try to quibble over my fees. And that, in my opinion, is what every salesperson should be aiming for. Whether you sell insurance or industrial equipment doesn't matter. Having a steady stream of happy people who want to buy from you will make your job, and your life, much easier.

It's always easy to tell a salesperson who is selling value to their clients from one who isn't. Over time, those who go the extra mile find themselves with more clients, higher margins, better relationships and making fewer cold calls. If you're managing your career the right way, you can build a solid career, and paycheck, instead of starting over every week.

To think of it a different way, consider what happens to your sales career if you don't go the distance for your clients. Gone is all that trust, all those repeat clients. Instead of dealing with satisfied customers who wouldn't think of working with anyone else, you're forced to prospect constantly to find new contacts to sell to. Rather than increasing your production with regular orders, each sale must start from the very beginning. Worse yet, clients that you've sold to in the past may not feel that you have their best interests at heart, meaning that they won't just avoid you, but may advise others to do so. None of this is to be taken lightly. Poor service and follow-up to your customer base can ruin your career. It's the sales version of a scorched earth policy. Keep this in mind and take care of those who buy from you. Don't sacrifice tomorrow's sale for a few minutes today.

So much of this book has been about what you can do for your sales career – better prospecting, qualifying and closing to bring in higher numbers – but don't overlook the ways that you can help yourself by helping your customers. When you create a lasting value for the customer, you aren't just doing the right thing – you're making your job a lot easier.

> **Be your own sales manager.**
> Take control of your career
> and don't rely on someone else to tell you
> what to do to increase your production.

The Greatest Sales Manager in the World

Earlier in this book, I described personality assessments and what they tell us about the makeup of great salespeople. There is obviously a lot to take away from their findings, but the story doesn't end there. After figuring out what makes top producers tick, researchers at TTI moved their attention up the food chain. What they found is that the highest producing salespeople seemed to come hand-in-hand with effective leadership. It was rare to have one without the other. With this observation in hand, they went on to take a closer look at sales managers and supervisors to see what their contributions were.

They learned that successful sales managers are able to help their sales team in a lot of ways. For starters, they tend to be great communicators. Whether it's a new policy, a bit of product knowledge, or some other piece of information, they're able to convey it to others in a way that is clear and succinct. By including important details without dwelling on the arcane, they are able to hold a listener's attention for long enough to make their point without drifting off into ideas that are irrelevant.

They're also masters of goal setting. Like top producers, they see an outcome and focus on it daily until it's been reached. This shouldn't be surprising. Ultimately, nearly all great sales are a result of having a good system, and working it consistently to hit targets. They know that small targets can turn into bigger targets, and that the only way to hit bigger goals is to hit all the smaller ones along the way. By manipulating their daily and weekly goals, they can guide producers to healthy and increasing annual figures.

Great managers understand the sales process, and know that each step is useful. Ask any of them, and they'll tell you that you can't skip any steps on route to a sale, and that to try means wasting time and energy. Without prospecting, you have no one to sell to. If the qualifying stage is rushed, you'll meet resistance when you close, and might experience problems after the sale. Closing itself must be done patiently, working with the client to overcome any fears or objections. For a sale to be made, all the pieces must fit. A strong manager will help his or her producers to keep this in mind, so that they aren't tempted to try to shortcut the selling process.

Another trait of top managers is that they understand the market for their products. They know where what they're selling fits in terms of price and quality, and use that knowledge to show clients the best options for a given situation. They can tell you anything you'd need to know about a product in their catalog, including its price and perceived strengths and weaknesses compared to the competition. This sort of thorough knowledge gives them the ability to coach their producers through presentations, as well as preparing them to counter objections.

Great managers know the value of expanding sales skills. They are always advising those under them to read another book or go to another seminar. They understand that training is never finished. Whatever you're selling today, somebody else is out there training to sell it better and to more people. You can't rely tomorrow on the same skills you used today. You have to keep learning or you will become stale. A strong supervisor will remind producers to keep training their minds and always be improving.

Another trait they have in common is focus. Have you ever noticed how sales managers are always focused on their quarterly numbers? That's not an accident. Simply put, great supervisors don't get distracted by what's going on around them. They know that they have a job to do – usually to help you hit a certain production goal – and will do whatever they can to help advance you to that point. Everything else should point in that direction, and they'll try to be sure that your activities reflect that.

And finally, they have patience. Most of them have been in sales long enough to know that there are going to be ups and downs. Being on top today doesn't mean that you'll necessarily be in the same place tomorrow. Likewise, a bad week, a bad month, or even a bad quarter can happen to anyone. Like coaches, they've seen the wins and losses, and know that quality work will succeed over time, and that the lazy and noncommittal will eventually wash out. They emphasize doing the right things every day, because they know that over time, you'll be successful that way.

Have you noticed anything about these traits? Two things should jump out in your mind. First, these are the same traits that top producers have, the ones we've talked about all through these pages. Second, these are all things that you can do for yourself.

Viewed in this light, it's no mystery why top producers and top managers go together. The best salespeople are the ones who don't need much supervision at all. Because they're motivated, focused, knowledgeable and patient, they simply go about doing what they need to do to make sales. They don't need anyone to tell them to make their calls. They already know the value of ongoing training. They have learned a sales system and are working it continually to perfection. They do their jobs so well that they routinely out-earn their colleagues, while requiring very little management.

That simple idea cuts to the heart of making it big in sales. It can be a lot of fun, but it's not a hand-holding business. Your manager can be a valuable resource, and you should take advantage of their knowledge and wisdom. But don't lean on them to write your paycheck, only you can do that. Be the kind of producer you'd want to manage. Give them a break and go to them when you need help, not because you want to put off your work or have someone do it for you. If you need someone to tell you what to do each day, then you aren't going to make it very far. But if you can find the drive and the fire within yourself, the path to success isn't a secret.

If you truly want to succeed in sales, if you want the money, the recognition, the thrill of being a top producer, then take it upon yourself to become one. Learn and master the techniques in this book, and then go out and find new ones for yourself. Read more, go to seminars, meet people. Don't procrastinate, and don't wait for someone else to tell you to do it. Take control of your own destiny.

You don't need someone to watch over you. The greatest sales manager in the world isn't sitting in another office of your building, or any other for that matter. It's you. Realize that, and you'll be well on the way to becoming a top producer.

It's in you to become more than you ever dreamed. Now, go out into the world and make it happen.

To order additional copies of this book
contact:

Henry Associates
704-847-7390
9430 Valley Road
Charlotte, NC 28270.
chenry@carlhenry.com
www.carlhenry.com